The Copilot Compass

Navigating Copilot and Agents in Microsoft 365

April Dunnam

apress®

The Copilot Compass: Navigating Copilot and Agents in Microsoft 365

April Dunnam
Broken Arrow, OK, USA

ISBN-13 (pbk): 979-8-8688-2654-2   ISBN-13 (electronic): 979-8-8688-2655-9
https://doi.org/10.1007/979-8-8688-2655-9

Managing Director, Apress Media LLC: Welmoed Spahr
Acquisitions Editor: Smriti Srivastava
Development Editor: Laura Berendson
Editorial Assistant: Marina Engler

Cover designed by eStudioCalamar

Distributed to the book trade worldwide by Springer Science+Business Media New York, 1 New York Plaza, New York, NY 10004. Phone 1-800-SPRINGER, fax (201) 348-4505, e-mail orders-ny@springer-sbm.com, or visit www.springeronline.com. Apress Media, LLC is a Delaware LLC and the sole member (owner) is Springer Science + Business Media Finance Inc (SSBM Finance Inc). SSBM Finance Inc is a **Delaware** corporation.

For information on translations, please e-mail booktranslations@springernature.com; for reprint, paperback, or audio rights, please e-mail bookpermissions@springernature.com.

Apress titles may be purchased in bulk for academic, corporate, or promotional use. eBook versions and licenses are also available for most titles. For more information, reference our Print and eBook Bulk Sales web page at http://www.apress.com/bulk-sales.

Any source code or other supplementary material referenced by the author in this book is available to readers on GitHub. For more detailed information, please visit https://www.apress.com/gp/services/source-code.

If disposing of this product, please recycle the paper

Table of Contents

About the Author xiii

About the Technical Reviewer xv

Acknowledgments xvii

Introduction xix

Chapter 1: The Copilot Confusion 1

The Origin Story 1

    Copilot Is the UI for AI 2

Why There Isn't Just One Copilot 3

    Same Interface, Different Boundaries.....................................3

    Standardization Doesn't Mean Simplification.........................4

    From One Name to Multiple Experiences 5

    Microsoft Copilot: General-Purpose AI...................................6

    Copilot Chat: Secure, but Not Grounded in Your Work..........7

    Microsoft 365 Copilot: Grounded in Your Organization's Context 8

    A Quick Note on Licensing...9

    A Quick Tour of Other Copilot Experiences 10

Copilot in Microsoft 365 11

    A Day in the Life of Using Copilot 12

Copilot and Agents: The Generalist and the Specialist.............13

    Low-Code First, On Purpose 15

Exploring Your Agent Options 15

A Decision Framework 17

Summary and Key Takeaways 18

Chapter 2: How Copilot Works **21**

The Road to Copilot 22

The Rule-Based Era 22

The Machine Learning Revolution 24

Deep Learning Emergence 25

The Generative AI Breakthrough 26

Large Language Models Explained 29

The Learning Process 30

Emergent Capabilities 31

Why It Can Write Code and New Content 32

The Limits of Large Language Models 33

Understanding Hallucination 34

What Hallucination Looks Like in Practice 35

What to Do About It 36

Summary and Key Takeaways 37

Chapter 3: The Buzzword Decoder Ring **39**

Prompts: The Entry Point 40

Types of Prompts 40

How to Write a Good Prompt 42

Make the Problem You're Trying to Solve the Focus 43

Beware of the Prompt Spiral 44

Prompts vs. Instructions...45

Tokens: The Building Blocks of Language Models 46

How Tokens Flow Through the Model...46

Why Tokens Matter to You 47

Grounding: Making Copilot Smarter with Your Data 48

    How Grounding Works 48

    What Copilot Can and Can't Ground On 49

    Why This Matters 50

Models: The Engines Behind Copilot 51

    Orchestration: Copilot's Invisible Decision Engine 52

    What Orchestration Really Does 53

    Why Orchestration Matters 54

    How Orchestration Works: A Concrete Example 55

    Bringing It All Together 58

Summary and Key Takeaways 59

Chapter 4: Workflows, Chatbots, and Agents 61

Why Everything Feels Like a Chatbot....................................61

What Exactly Is Intent?...62

Chatbots: Different Kinds, Different Capabilities 63

    Traditional Chatbots..64

    AI Chatbots: Conversation Powered by Large Language Models..................65

    What Chatbots Do and Don't Do 66

Workflows: Execution Without Interpretation 66

AI Automation: Adding More Intelligence to Workflows............67

Agents: Reasoning Inside the System 68

Determinism Dictates Approach 69

Agents and Workflows Together...70

    Why Agent Flows Exist 71

    Revisiting an Earlier Scenario 71

TABLE OF CONTENTS

Addressing Common Misconceptions 72

    Misconception #1: "Agents Are Just Workflows with AI" 72

    Misconception #2: "With AI, I Can Put All My Work on Autopilot" 73

    Misconception #3: "Putting AI on Everything Automatically Means Better Outcomes" 74

Choosing the Right Tool for the Job 74

    When a Chatbot Is Enough 75

    When You Need a Workflow 76

    When AI Automation Helps but Isn't Sufficient 76

    When You Need an Agent 77

    When You Don't Need an Agent 78

    When an App Is the Better Interface 79

    Apps and Agents Work Best Together 80

    Over-conversationalizing Work 81

    Combining Patterns Thoughtfully 81

One Scenario, Four Approaches 82

    Approach 1: Chatbot 82

    Approach 2: Workflow 83

    Approach 3: AI Automation (The Bridge) 83

    Approach 4: Agent 84

So, What Is Copilot, Really? 84

Summary and Key Takeaways 85

Chapter 5: The Agent Builder's Toolbox 87

Build vs. Use: Knowing When Not to Build an Agent 88

Understanding the Types of Agents You Can Build 89

    Retrieval-Based Agents 90

    Task-Based Agents 90

    Autonomous Agents 90

Declarative Agents: The Starting Point 91

    Why Declarative Agents Exist 92

    What "Declarative" Actually Means 93

    What You Gain by Letting Copilot Orchestrate 94

    Ways to Build Declarative Agents 95

    What All Declarative Tools Have in Common 98

    Why This Is the "Starting Point" 99

When Declarative Agents Start to Crack 99

    Signal 1: You Need Deterministic Workflow Control 100

    Signal 2: You Are Integrating Multiple Disparate Systems 100

    Signal 3: You Want Explicit Tool Invocation Beyond Declarative Actions 101

    Signal 4: Predictability Is Non-Negotiable 101

    Signal 5: You Are Repeating Complex Orchestration Logic
    Outside Copilot 102

    A Practical Rule of Thumb 102

Custom Engine Agents: When You Need to Take Control 103

    Why Custom Engine Agents Exist 103

    What "Custom Engine" Actually Means 104

    Practical Examples of Custom Engine Scenarios 104

    Low-Code vs. Pro-Code Custom Engines 106

    What You Trade When You Go Custom 107

    A Natural Transition Point 107

Copilot Studio: The Gateway Between Declarative and Custom
Engine Agents 108

    Copilot Studio and Declarative Agents 109

    Where Copilot Studio Becomes a Custom Engine Environment 109

    Deployment Inside Microsoft 365 and Beyond 110

    Bringing It All Together 111

When Pro-Code Becomes Necessary 111

    What "Pro-Code" Actually Means in This Context 111

    Why Low-Code Sometimes Hits a Ceiling 112

    Pro-Code Building Blocks in the Copilot Extensibility Model 113

    Copilot Connectors and Plugins 114

    Custom Services and External Orchestration 115

    What Changes When You Move to Pro-Code 116

    Pro-Code As a Strategic Choice, Not a Default 116

Decision Framework: Choosing the Right Tool 117

    Scenario 1: HR Policy and Benefits Questions 117

    Scenario 2: Sales Proposal Assistant 118

    Scenario 3: Employee Onboarding Task Coordinator 119

    Scenario 4: Finance Approval Agent 120

Summary and Key Takeaways 123

Chapter 6: Use Cases, Pitfalls, and the Road Ahead 125

What Actually Works: Lessons from Copilot in the Wild 126

    Pattern #1: The Expectation Trap 127

    Pattern #2: The Outcome Shift 128

    Pattern #3: Data Hygiene Is the Silent Killer 129

    Pattern #4: Security and Integration Decide the Ceiling 130

    Pattern #5: Communities Beat Training 132

    Pattern #6: What Gets Measured Gets Funded 134

Where Agents Earn Their Keep 136

The Copilot Adoption Maturity Curve 138

    Stage 1: Curiosity and Search 138

    Stage 2: Drafting and Content Acceleration 139

    Stage 3: Socialization and Standardization 140

Stage 4: Agent Experimentation and Guardrails 141

Stage 5: Operationalized Agents...142

The Road Ahead 144

AI As a Baseline Skill, Not a Specialty 144

Agents As Leverage, Not Replacements 145

Humans As Designers of Work Systems...146

A Realistic Future, Not a Magical One 147

Summary and Key Takeaways 149

Index...151

About the Author

April Dunnam is a Principal Cloud Advocate at Microsoft, where she helps thousands of professionals around the world understand and adopt low-code, AI, and automation technologies. With a background as a SharePoint and .NET developer, she brings a rare mix of deep technical expertise and an approachable teaching style that makes complex topics accessible to everyone.

April is an international speaker and YouTube creator. Her YouTube channel, followed by tens of thousands of makers and developers, is known for breaking down Microsoft Power Platform and AI concepts in a way that is practical, engaging, and easy to understand.

She has been at the forefront of the shift from apps and workflows to Copilot and AI agents, advising organizations and communities on how to use these new tools effectively. April is passionate about empowering people—whether they are business users, IT pros, or developers—to harness AI in ways that drive real impact.

When she is not creating content or speaking at events, you'll likely find her making music with her band or spending time with her family in Tulsa, Oklahoma.

About the Technical Reviewer

 **Kasam Shaikh** is a four-time recipient of the prestigious Microsoft Most Valuable Professional (MVP) Award in AI making him the first and only Indian professional under the age of 40 to earn this honor three times consecutively. A recognized Global AI Speaker, published author, and tech influencer, Kasam is widely known for his contributions to the AI ecosystem through his YouTube channel, mentoring initiatives, and thought leadership. He currently serves as an Apps and AI Architect, driving digital transformation and AI adoption across business units. As the founder of Dear Azure – Az-INDIA, the largest Azure AI community in the region, he plays a key role in nurturing AI talent and fostering innovation. Additionally, he is acknowledged as a Career Expert in AI by RediffGuru and leads the Gen AI Expert Community at the practice level within his organization.

Acknowledgments

I want to thank the many practitioners, builders, architects, and leaders who shared their experiences and perspectives with me while I was writing this book. Some asked to remain anonymous, and I respect that, but their stories and candor shaped this work in ways that can't be overstated.

Thank you to the communities around Microsoft Power Platform, Copilot Studio, and Microsoft 365 for constantly pushing the conversation forward and for generously sharing what you learn.

I'm also deeply grateful to the team at Apress for their guidance and patience throughout this process.

Finally, thank you to my partner for supporting me along the way, enduring countless late nights and conversations about agents that probably went on longer than anyone wanted.

Introduction

Right now, it's hard to tell what's real and what's hype when it comes to Copilot and AI agents.

Every week, there's a new announcement, a new demo, a new acronym, and a new bold prediction about how everything is about to change. Copilot, agents, large language models, orchestration, and autonomous AI are often used interchangeably, even though they mean very different things.

This book exists to cut through that noise.

It's not a step-by-step tutorial for building the most advanced AI solution possible. It's an exploration of what Copilot and agents actually are, how they work, what they're good at, and where they fall short, so you can make better decisions about how to use them.

Over the last few years, the way we build and use software has started to shift. Instead of relying solely on screens, forms, and workflows, people increasingly expect to interact with systems through natural language. They want to ask questions, get summaries, generate content, and take action without needing to understand every underlying system.

That expectation is reshaping how applications are designed.

It's also reshaping what it means to be a builder, a technologist, or even a knowledge worker.

You don't need to become a machine learning expert to participate in this shift. But you do need a basic understanding for how these systems behave.

Without that, it's easy to overestimate what AI can do. It's just as easy to underestimate it.

This book focuses on building that understanding.

You'll learn how large language models generate responses, what an agent actually is, and how orchestration connects AI to real systems. More importantly, you'll learn how these pieces fit together inside Copilot.

Throughout the book, the emphasis stays practical.

Not "copy this code."

Not "follow this exact recipe."

Instead: "Here's how to think about this problem."

Who This Book Is For

This book is written for

- Business users who want to understand Copilot beyond surface-level features

- Makers and developers building solutions with Power Platform and Microsoft 365

- IT and platform teams responsible for governance, security, and enablement

- Leaders trying to separate signal from noise

If you've ever wondered when to use a workflow versus an agent, why prompts sometimes work and sometimes don't, or what "autonomous" really means in practice, you're in the right place.

What Makes This Book Different

Most AI books fall into one of two categories. They're either deeply technical and focused on model architecture and training. Or they're high-level and focused on big-picture vision.

This book lives in between.

It focuses on how AI shows up in real tools, inside real organizations, used by real people.

You'll see patterns, trade-offs, and common failure modes. You'll see why data quality matters more than clever prompts, why guardrails matter more than raw capability, and why humans remain firmly in the loop.

The goal isn't to make you an AI expert.

The goal is to make you a confident decision-maker.

How This Book Is Structured

Part I introduces core concepts: large language models, Copilot, agents, and the mental models you'll use throughout the book.

Part II explores building blocks and patterns, including prompting, grounding, tools, and orchestration.

Part III focuses on applying these ideas in real scenarios and organizations.

The final chapter brings everything together with practical patterns, a maturity model, and a realistic view of where things are heading.

Each chapter is designed to stand on its own, but they build on each other.

You don't need to read this book cover to cover in order. But if you do, you'll gradually develop a clearer map of the Copilot and agent landscape.

My goal with this book is simple: to help you understand Copilot enough to use it intentionally.

Let's get started.

Because AI tools are evolving rapidly, product names, features, and capabilities may change over time. The concepts in this book are designed to give you a good understanding of Copilot and agents, even as specific features and terminology continue to evolve.

CHAPTER 1

The Copilot Confusion

If it feels like the word *Copilot* is everywhere, you're not imagining it. Over the last few years, Microsoft has associated the Copilot name with tools across Word, Excel, PowerPoint, Windows, and beyond. For many of us, this Copilot explosion has created a simple but frustrating question:

Which Copilot should I use and when?

That question is more complex than it looks, because Copilot isn't a single tool. It's something broader, applied across many products in slightly different ways. Understanding what Copilot is and how agents extend it is the first step toward using it effectively rather than feeling overwhelmed by it.

This chapter is about orientation. You'll learn how Copilot shows up across Microsoft 365, how agents fit into the picture, and why choosing the *right* level of automation matters just as much as using AI at all.

The Origin Story

The Copilot origin story goes back to 2021, with the launch of GitHub Copilot. At the time, AI assistants weren't truly mainstream. Siri and Alexa had been around for a while, but they felt more like novelty personal assistants than serious work partners.

© April Dunnam 2026

A. Dunnam, *The Copilot Compass*, https://doi.org/10.1007/979-8-8688-2655-9_1

GitHub Copilot was different. It lived directly inside your coding environment and suggested code as developers worked. It wasn't perfect, but it was surprisingly helpful and, more importantly, it reduced friction. Developers could stay focused on solving problems instead of getting bogged down by syntax and repetitive code. It was like having a junior developer teammate. It didn't replace the need for senior developers to architect solutions, review code, or make strategic decisions. But it eliminated much of the tedious, repetitive work that slows down development.

The name *Copilot* was chosen deliberately. When you're working, whether you're writing code, building a presentation, or analyzing data, you are the pilot. You're in the proverbial cockpit, making decisions and steering the outcome. A Copilot doesn't replace that role. It supports it. It's there to support you, reduce friction, and help you move faster. That framing is key because when you understand that Copilot is a tool designed to work *with* you rather than *instead of* you, it's empowering.

Copilot Is the UI for AI

Microsoft often describes Copilot as *"the UI for AI."* That phrase is deceptively simple, but it captures something important. AI by itself can feel abstract, like it's just a giant model out in the cloud somewhere doing magical things. But this phrase captures what Copilot actually represents.

Copilot isn't a stand-alone application or a single feature. It's Microsoft's standardized way of presenting AI inside the tools people already use to get work done. Instead of asking users to leave Word, Excel, or Teams to interact with an AI system, Copilot brings AI directly into those experiences.

In that sense, Copilot is a **shared AI experience layer**. It defines how people interact with AI through conversational prompts, contextual suggestions, and guided actions while sitting on top of underlying models, services, and data sources.

This is why Copilot can appear in so many places and still feel familiar. The interface and interaction style remain largely consistent, even though what Copilot can access and what it's allowed to do varies by product, license, and context.

Why There Isn't Just One Copilot

At first glance, it feels like there should be just one Copilot.

After all, the interface looks familiar no matter where you encounter it. You type a prompt, Copilot responds. Whether you're in a browser, inside Word, or working in Teams, the experience feels consistent. But under the surface, these Copilot experiences operate under different rules.

The reason there isn't just one Copilot comes down to boundaries, specifically, what Copilot is allowed to know and what it's allowed to do.

Same Interface, Different Boundaries

One of the most confusing aspects of Copilot is that two experiences can look nearly identical and behave very differently.

In one context, Copilot might answer a question using general knowledge from the web. In another, it might reference your emails, your documents, or your meeting history. In a third, it may deliberately avoid accessing any organizational data at all.

From a user's perspective, it feels inconsistent. From a platform perspective, it's essential.

Different Copilot experiences exist because different scenarios carry different levels of risk. Helping someone brainstorm a personal project is fundamentally different from helping someone analyze internal financial data. The same AI behavior that feels helpful in one context could be dangerous in another if applied without the right safeguards.

That's why Microsoft draws clear lines between Copilot experiences, even when the interface is shared.

Standardization Doesn't Mean Simplification

To be fair, Microsoft has made real progress toward standardizing the Copilot experience across products.

In Microsoft 365 apps like Word, Excel, PowerPoint, Outlook, and even Power Apps, Copilot is increasingly presented through a consistent interface and interaction model. This is great because it reduces friction and helps Copilot feel like a cohesive part of the platform rather than a collection of disconnected features.

More recently, Microsoft has also begun introducing agents directly into this same Microsoft 365 Copilot experience. Word, Excel, and PowerPoint agents, for example, live alongside Copilot and extend it, rather than existing as separate tools. From a user perspective, this reinforces the idea that there is a single, unified Copilot experience across Microsoft 365.

And that's mostly true within that ecosystem.

What this standardization doesn't mean is that every Copilot-branded experience behaves the same way everywhere.

Some Copilot experiences are part of the Microsoft 365 Copilot platform and operate under enterprise identity, permissions, and governance. Others use the Copilot name but exist entirely outside that platform. They may share design patterns or conversational interfaces, but they don't share the same data boundaries, security model, or extensibility options.

This is where confusion still creeps in.

When Copilot appears in many places and looks the same, it's easy to assume it's the same system underneath. In reality, the interface may be standardized, while the rules behind it are not. Understanding which Copilot experiences are part of the Microsoft 365 Copilot platform and which aren't is more important than memorizing where Copilot appears.

From One Name to Multiple Experiences

All of this leads to an important conclusion: there isn't just one Copilot because there isn't just one set of boundaries.

Rather than offering a single AI experience that tries to work everywhere, Microsoft has taken a layered approach. Each Copilot experience is designed around a different level of context, trust, and responsibility. As you move from one to another, what changes isn't the interface; it's what Copilot is allowed to know, what it's allowed to act on, and what safeguards are in place.

Instead of thinking of Copilot as a single product, it's more accurate to view it as a shared AI capability expressed through multiple experiences, each optimized for a specific scenario. Those experiences may look similar on the surface, but they serve very different purposes.

At a high level, Microsoft Copilot shows up in three primary ways:

- Copilot, a consumer-focused experience designed for personal, everyday use

- Copilot Chat, which brings enterprise-grade security to AI-assisted work without grounding responses in organizational data

- Microsoft 365 Copilot, which is deeply grounded in your organization's files, emails, meetings, and business context

You can think of these Copilot experiences as concentric circles, with each layer bringing Copilot closer to your work and increasing the level of responsibility that comes with it (Figure 1-1).

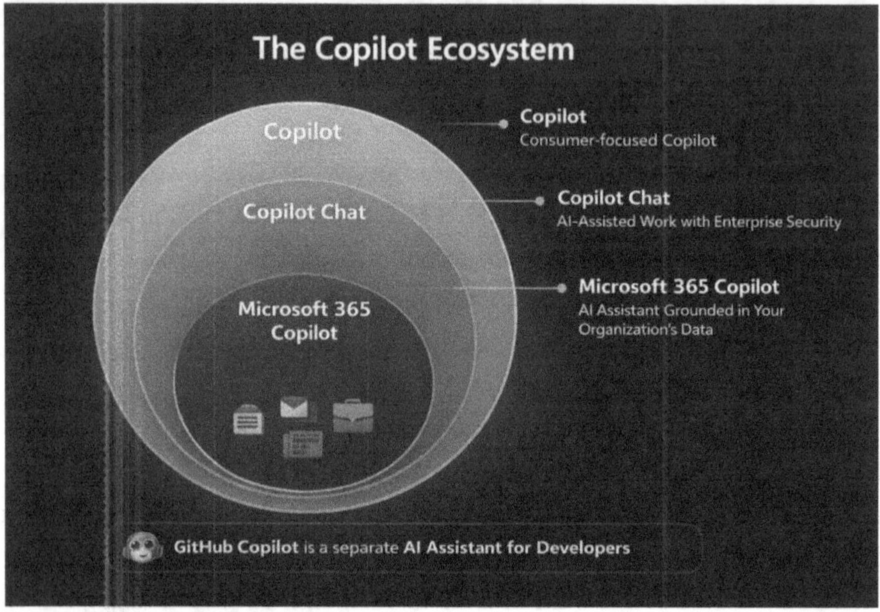

Figure 1-1. *The Copilot Ecosystem*

In the sections that follow, we'll walk through each of these Copilot experiences in detail, starting with the most general and moving toward the most context aware.

Microsoft Copilot: General-Purpose AI

At the outermost layer is **Copilot for personal use**, often referred to simply as Microsoft Copilot. If you're familiar with ChatGPT, this is the closest Microsoft equivalent. It offers a general-purpose AI assistant designed for everyday, personal use rather than organizational work. It's grounded in general web knowledge and public information, and it has no awareness of your organization, your files, or your work context.

Like ChatGPT, it comes in a free tier and a paid tier. The free version gives you access to the core AI experience, while the paid tier adds priority access to the latest models, faster performance, and enhanced capabilities.

The free version is a great starting point, and many people find it more than sufficient for everyday tasks.

Copilot is great for brainstorming, drafting personal content, or answering general questions, but it should never be used with sensitive or proprietary work information. There is no organizational context or governance applied here.

Copilot Chat: Secure, but Not Grounded in Your Work

Copilot Chat introduces a vital shift: **enterprise-grade security**.

This version is designed for work scenarios where you want AI assistance without exposing organizational data. It can help with brainstorming, research, summarization, drafting, and ideation, but it doesn't automatically ground its responses in your emails, files, meetings, or internal documents. It knows what's on the internet. It doesn't know what's in your SharePoint.

Think of Copilot Chat as a safe, secure way to use AI *at work*, without giving it access to your work.

Let's look at a few scenarios where Copilot Chat might be the right tool over the consumer Copilot experience:

- A consultant wants to brainstorm a client presentation structure without risking any internal data being exposed to an unsecured AI system.

- A manager wants to use AI to summarize a public industry report they've pasted into the chat window.

- A new employee wants to experiment with Copilot and get comfortable with prompting before their organization rolls out full Microsoft 365 Copilot licenses.

In each case, Copilot Chat provides real value without requiring the deeper integration, governance configuration, or licensing that Microsoft 365 Copilot demands.

This makes it a natural starting point for organizations that want to enable AI broadly while keeping data boundaries tight. It's also why many organizations deploy Copilot Chat first, using it as a proving ground before expanding to Microsoft 365 Copilot for users who need deeper organizational context.

Microsoft 365 Copilot: Grounded in Your Organization's Context

Microsoft 365 Copilot is where the experience changes significantly.

In this mode, Copilot is allowed to ground its responses in your organization's data within the permissions you already have. It can reference your emails, documents, meetings, chats, and calendar to provide answers that are specific to *your* work, not just work in general.

This grounding is what makes Microsoft 365 Copilot powerful and also what makes governance essential. Because Microsoft 365 Copilot is operating inside your work context, it must respect identity, permissions, and compliance requirements.

The interface may look familiar, but the **security model is completely different**.

Here's a simple way to keep them straight (Table 1-1).

Table 1-1. *Types of Copilot Experiences*

What you want	Which Copilot	Where to find it	What it knows
Personal help	Microsoft Copilot	copilot.microsoft.com	The internet
Secure brainstorming	Microsoft 365 Copilot Chat	m365copilot.com	The internet + enterprise security
Work with your data	Microsoft 365 Copilot	Microsoft 365 apps + m365.cloud.microsoft	The internet + enterprise security + your organization's data

A Quick Note on Licensing

One final layer that influences how Copilot behaves is **licensing**.

Different Copilot experiences are enabled through different subscriptions. Features that ground Copilot in your organization's data or allow agents to act on your behalf require additional licensing beyond basic access to Copilot Chat or consumer Copilot experiences.

Because we all know that licensing models evolve over time, we're going to avoid listing out specific SKUs and pricing. Instead, we will focus on helping you understand *what's possible* and *which questions to ask* when evaluating whether a particular Copilot or agent capability is available in your environment.

If your Copilot experience looks different from examples in this book, licensing is often the reason.

A Quick Tour of Other Copilot Experiences

Microsoft uses the Copilot name across a growing number of products. While this book focuses on Microsoft 365 Copilot and agents, it's helpful to understand what other Copilot experiences exist and what they're designed to do.

- **Copilot in Power Platform** helps makers describe an app, website, or automation in natural language and generates a starting point for low-code applications and workflows. It's designed to lower the barrier to building business apps.

- **Security Copilot** is built for security professionals to investigate incidents, summarize alerts, streamline security tasks, and analyze security data.

- **Dynamics 365 Copilot** appears within business applications such as Sales and Customer Service, where it helps summarize records, draft communications, and surface insights from CRM data.

- **Windows Copilot** brings AI assistance into the operating system itself, focusing on settings, search, and general productivity tasks on your device.

- **GitHub Copilot** supports developers by assisting with code, tests, and documentation directly inside development environments.

Each of these Copilot experiences follows the same broad idea of bringing AI into the flow of work, but they operate in different domains, with various data, risks, and audiences.

In this book, we'll focus on **Microsoft 365 Copilot** because it sits at the intersection of everyday work, organizational data, agents, and governance. The concepts you'll learn apply broadly, even when the tools differ.

Copilot in Microsoft 365

Within Microsoft 365, Copilot appears directly within familiar apps like Word, Excel, PowerPoint, Outlook, Teams, and SharePoint. These in-context experiences are designed to help you work more efficiently.

You might use Copilot in Word to expand a draft document, in Excel to generate or explain a formula, or in Outlook to summarize a long email thread. In each case, Copilot responds to what you ask and helps you save time while you remain in control.

These experiences are intentionally **assistive**. Copilot suggests, drafts, and summarizes, but it doesn't decide what work should happen next. That distinction becomes important when we start talking about agents.

Microsoft 365 Copilot doesn't rely solely on the model's general knowledge. It has a built-in intelligence layer, Work IQ, that integrates with your work data and considers users' roles, tasks, and organizational context. Work IQ provides a behind-the-scenes map of your work life, connecting your meetings, emails, files, chats, and calendar to make Microsoft 365 Copilot context-aware. It has the power of inference and memory to understand the difference between a marketing campaign report you worked on yesterday and a sales forecast your colleague shared with you this morning. It can bring those threads together because it lives in the same ecosystem where your work happens.

Think of Microsoft 365 like a city. The apps are the buildings where you get things done. Work IQ is the infrastructure, the roads, bridges, and power lines connecting everything. And Copilot is the assistant who can navigate the city for you, bringing what you need, when you need it.

A Day in the Life of Using Copilot

Consider a Monday morning. You return from an entirely too short weekend to find 50 unread emails and three meetings before noon.

You open Outlook and ask Copilot to summarize what needs your attention. In a few seconds, it surfaces the three threads that require a response, flags a deadline you nearly missed, and drafts a reply to your manager for you to review based on the email chain context.

You move to Word, where a report draft is waiting for your revisions. You ask Copilot to tighten the executive summary and adjust the tone for a senior leadership audience. It does both in under a minute.

Before your first meeting, you open Teams and ask Copilot to recap the key decisions from last Thursday's call that you couldn't attend. It pulls the meeting transcript, identifies the action items assigned to you, and surfaces a document your colleague shared during the discussion.

None of these interactions required you to leave the apps you were already in. None required a special command or technical knowledge. You asked, in plain language, and Copilot responded in context.

That's the daily experience this book is designed to help you use well.

Note Clearing up misconceptions   Before we go further, it's worth addressing two assumptions that tend to get in the way when it comes to Copilot. Clearing these up early will help you get more out of everything that follows.

1. **Copilot isn't "just a search engine."** When you type a question into Copilot, it doesn't retrieve a ranked list of web pages and surface the best one, as a traditional search engine would. It generates a response based on patterns learned during training, combined with whatever grounding data is available in your context. We'll explore this more in upcoming chapters.

2. **Copilot doesn't give you blanket access to everything in your organization.** Microsoft 365 Copilot always respects your permissions. If you can't open a file in SharePoint, Copilot can't read it either. If a Teams channel is private and you're not a member, Copilot won't surface content from it. This is an important safeguard because it means Copilot cannot inadvertently expose data you weren't supposed to see. It also means that if Copilot seems unaware of something you know exists in your organization, a permissions or configuration gap is often the explanation.

Copilot and Agents: The Generalist and the Specialist

Think of Copilot as your primary care doctor. It's a generalist that can help you with many tasks. But you wouldn't go to your primary care for eye surgery; you would go to a specialist for that.

Agents are your specialists. They're designed to focus on a narrower domain but go much deeper within it. For example, the **Analyst Agent** is specifically trained to work with your data, run analysis, and give insights. That's all it does, and it does it well.

The power of Microsoft 365 Copilot is that it gives you both. You get the generalist Copilot embedded directly where you work, and you also gain access to specialist agents that can take on more complex, domain-specific tasks. Even better, Microsoft gives you the tools to **host, customize, and build your own agents**. With **Copilot Studio**, you can create custom agents tailored to your business; whether that's an HR agent that helps onboard new employees or a compliance agent that checks documents against company policy.

Most teams don't start out thinking they need agents. They start by asking Copilot for help: summarizing documents, drafting emails, and preparing for meetings. At first, that assistance is enough.

But over time, patterns emerge.

The same questions get asked.

The same steps are repeated.

That's when teams begin to realize they're not just asking for help, they're redoing execution.

This is where specialists come in. Agents are designed to handle well-defined tasks end to end, especially when the work is repeatable and the desired outcome is clear.

And here's where the fundamental distinction between Copilot and an agent becomes clear: Copilot operates on a "you ask, it responds" model. You provide a prompt, and it returns an answer or a draft. An agent, on the other hand, can reason, plan, and act on your behalf. It doesn't just hand you a result; it can follow a sequence of steps, integrate with tools, and execute a process from start to finish.

In other words, Copilot helps you get work done faster. Agents can do the work for you.

Moving from a generalist (Copilot) to a specialist (agent) is also a shift in responsibility. When you ask an agent to act on your behalf, you're delegating decisions. That makes boundaries, permissions, and oversight essential, not optional.

The most effective implementations don't replace Copilot with agents. They layer them. Copilot remains the generalist in the flow of work, while agents handle execution where intent is clear, outcomes are repeatable, and the risk is understood.

Low-Code First, On Purpose

Microsoft provides multiple ways to create agents. In this book, Copilot Studio serves as the primary example, not because it's the only option but because it's the most accessible starting point for most people.

Low-code tools allow people close to the work to experiment, iterate, and deliver value quickly without over-engineering solutions. They're well-suited for repeatable questions, team-level workflows, and scenarios where intent and boundaries are well understood.

More advanced approaches exist for situations that require deeper control, custom orchestration, or specialized integrations. You don't need to master those tools to understand when they're appropriate.

What matters most is developing the judgment to choose the right level of tooling for the problem you're trying to solve.

Exploring Your Agent Options

Understanding agents conceptually is one thing, but let's talk about what this looks like inside Microsoft 365 Copilot. You'll find two primary types of agents: pre-built agents that are immediately useful, and custom agents that you can design to match your business processes.

Pre-Built Agents are the ones Microsoft (or other 3rd party companies) have designed and tuned for you. They're specialists that come ready out of the box with little to no setup. For example, the **Researcher Agent** can help you dig up background material and synthesize information from your files and the web. The **Canva Agent enables you to create new designs and visuals directly in M365 Copilot.**

But every business is unique, and sometimes you need an agent that is specific to your unique scenario, and that's where custom agents come in. Microsoft gives you two paths here, depending on how complex your needs are:

- **Agent Builder**: A low-code interface inside Microsoft 365 Copilot that lets you quickly spin up agents without writing any code. Perfect for lightweight specialists, like an HR agent that answers policy questions.

- **Copilot Studio**: A more advanced toolkit where you can build agents that integrate with external systems, connect to APIs through MCP Servers (a standard for connecting AI to external tools and services), or carry out more sophisticated logic. For example, IT could use Copilot Studio to create an agent that triages helpdesk requests by checking system status, walking a user through troubleshooting steps, and even making a ticket in the backend system or escalating to a live technician if needed. Or a sales team could design an agent that pulls customer data from a CRM, surfaces relevant history, and helps prep for a big pitch.

This is where Microsoft's ecosystem shines. Copilot isn't just about personal productivity; it's also about organizational productivity. It enables companies to design intelligent assistants that not only answer questions but also actively support business processes.

Let's look at some real-world examples of custom agents you might build with Copilot Studio.

HR Policy Agent: An employee asks: "What's our remote work policy for international travel?" The HR agent searches through policy documents, finds relevant sections about remote work and international considerations, and provides a comprehensive answer, including approval processes, tax implications, and IT security requirements.

Sales Enablement Agent: A sales rep preparing for a client meeting asks: "Show me our latest case studies for retail companies and any recent wins in the fashion industry." The agent searches through sales collateral, recent presentations, and CRM data to compile relevant materials and even suggests talking points based on the prospect's industry challenges.

IT Support Agent: When someone reports, "My laptop won't connect to the VPN, and I have an important client call in 30 minutes," the IT agent can

1. Check the user's device status and recent network changes

2. Provide step-by-step troubleshooting instructions

3. Suggest creating a support ticket or escalating to a live technician if automated steps don't work

Pre-built agents give you a fast on-ramp, while the custom agents give you unlimited potential. Together, they transform Copilot from a personal helper into an enterprise-wide network of specialists that can reason, plan, and act on behalf of your teams.

A Decision Framework

When deciding how to use Copilot or whether to introduce an agent, start with three questions (Figure 1-2):

1. **Am I exploring or executing?**

    Copilot is ideal for exploration, drafting, and sense-making. Agents shine when execution becomes repeatable.

2. **Who is this for, and how often does it happen?**

    One-off, personal tasks rarely need an agent. Team-wide, recurring work often does.

3. **What's the risk if this goes wrong?**

    The higher the impact, the more critical permissions, approvals, and oversight become.

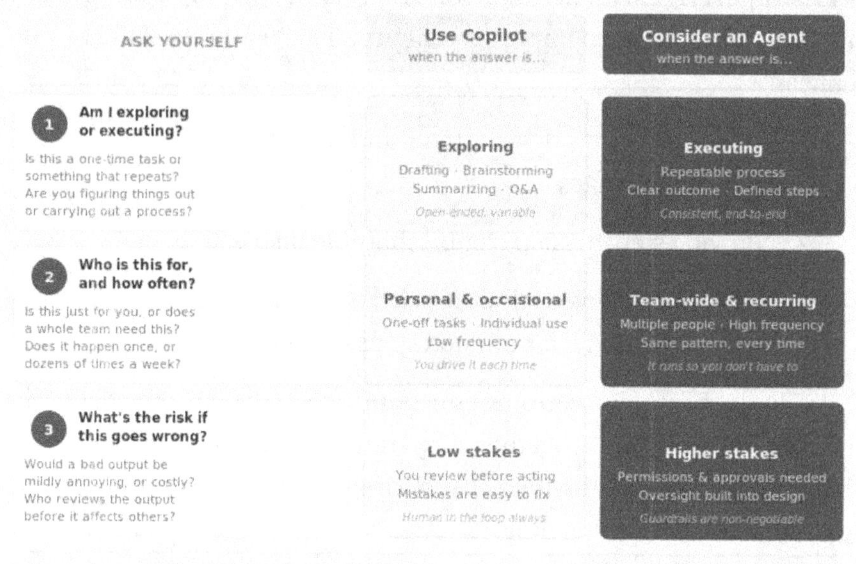

Figure 1-2. *A Decision Framework*

Many teams struggle not because Copilot is ineffective, but because they apply the wrong tool to the problem. This framework helps you avoid both underusing AI and overengineering solutions.

Without a clear framework, it's easy to get lost in the noise. I've seen teams waste weeks treating Copilot like a glorified search engine. Spoiler: it's not. Others overengineer by building custom agents when a pre-built SharePoint Agent could have done the job.

Summary and Key Takeaways

The term Copilot has been applied across many Microsoft products. This chapter provided the orientation needed to navigate this Copilot landscape with confidence.

Rather than treating Copilot as a single tool, you've seen how it functions as a shared AI experience that shows up in different contexts, with different permissions, data access, and responsibilities. Understanding these distinctions is essential before diving deeper into how Copilot works.

Key takeaways from this chapter:

- Copilot is Microsoft's AI user experience layer, not a single product.

- Microsoft 365 Copilot focuses on work grounded in organizational context.

- Copilot is assistive by design; agents specialize and can act.

- Low-code tools are the right starting point for most agent scenarios.

- Applying the right tool to the right problem. Copilot for exploration, agents for execution, is where most teams find sustained value

Now that you have a map of the Copilot landscape, the next step is understanding what's happening under the hood. In Chapter 2, we'll demystify how large language models work and how they power Copilot.

CHAPTER 2

How Copilot Works

When people talk about Copilot, you'll often hear two extreme takes. On one end of the spectrum, there's the hype: *"It's magic. It understands everything."* On the other hand, there's dismissal: *"It's just fancy autocomplete."*

The truth is somewhere in the middle.

To use Copilot effectively, you need a basic understanding of what's happening under the hood. That doesn't mean becoming an AI engineer. But if you can wrap your head around the basics, you'll start to see why Copilot feels so powerful, where its limits are, and why it's not magic at all, it's math.

This chapter focuses on the foundation: **large language models (LLMs)**. You'll learn how modern AI evolved from rule-based systems to ultimately generative AI. We'll explain how LLMs are trained, what they actually do when they generate text, and why they can sound confident, even when they're wrong.

What we will *not* cover in depth here is how Microsoft wires these models into Copilot, how grounding and orchestration work, or how agents act on your behalf. Those concepts build on the foundation you'll learn in this chapter and are explored in the chapters that follow.

By the end of this chapter, you should have a clear mental model of what LLMs are, what they're good at, where their limits are, and why Copilot behaves the way it does. That understanding is essential before we move on to buzzwords, tooling, and real-world use cases.

© April Dunnam 2026

A. Dunnam, *The Copilot Compass*, https://doi.org/10.1007/979-8-8688-2655-9_2

The Road to Copilot

You might view Copilot and the recent surge in generative AI as an overnight success that took the world by storm. But like most breakthroughs, it's the product of decades of steady progress.

AI's roots stretch back to the 1950s, when Alan Turing posed his famous question: "Can machines think?" In his landmark paper, he described the Turing Test, a method for measuring a machine's ability to mimic human conversation. That idea led to early experiments in symbolic AI, in which researchers sought to hard-code logic and reasoning into machines.

The journey since then hasn't followed a straight line. AI has moved through cycles of optimism and setbacks, with each wave of progress fueled by new approaches.

The Rule-Based Era

Back in "the late 1900s," as the kids like to call it (the 1980s and 1990s in this case), artificial intelligence looked very different from what it is today. Most AI systems were built like elaborate decision trees with massive collections of "if-then" rules that programmers had to write. These were called **expert systems**, and they represented the state of the art in AI technology at the time.

The concept was straightforward: capture human expertise by reducing it to logical rules. If a bank loan applicant has income above $50,000 and good credit, then approve the loan. If someone calls the help desk about email problems, then walk them through the standard troubleshooting checklist.

The problem with this approach was that every piece of knowledge had to be painstakingly and explicitly programmed.

Consider what this meant for something like a help desk system. Programmers would need to anticipate every possible way someone might describe their problem:

- "My computer won't start."

- "I have the blue screen of death."

- "Nothing happens when I press the power button."

- "My PC is dead."

- "The machine isn't responding."

Each variation required its own rule or pattern match. Miss a variation, and the user would hit a dead end because the system didn't know how to respond to anything outside its programmed knowledge.

This made the systems very brittle because they couldn't learn from experience, adapt to new situations, or handle ambiguity. When the business changed, the software required manual updates. When users found new ways to describe problems, programmers had to add new rules.

By the 1990s, it became clear that this approach had fundamental limitations. You couldn't manually encode all human knowledge, and even if you could, maintaining those systems was a nightmare.

What these early systems lacked was the ability to generalize, to take what they learned in one context and apply it to new, similar situations. They were intelligent within their programmed boundaries, but completely helpless outside them.

This limitation persisted until the early aughts, when a fundamentally new approach emerged.

The Machine Learning Revolution

The early 2000s brought a shift in how we think about artificial intelligence. Instead of trying to hard-code human expertise into rules, researchers began asking a different question: What if we could teach computers to learn patterns from examples?

This was the dawn of practical **machine learning**. Rather than a programmer sitting down to write "if the customer says, 'password reset,' then show form A," you could feed a system thousands of actual customer service interactions and let it discover the patterns on its own. Show it enough examples of emails labeled "urgent" or "immediate action," and it would learn to classify new emails automatically.

The breakthrough was profound because you no longer needed to anticipate every possible way someone might phrase a request. The system could generalize from examples, handling variations it had never seen before. If it learned from examples like "I can't get into my account" and "Login isn't working," it might correctly handle "Unable to access my profile," even if that exact phrase wasn't in the training data.

Machine learning powered the first wave of practical AI applications that we still use today, like

> **Spam filters that actually worked**: Email providers could finally distinguish between legitimate messages and junk mail by learning from millions of examples, rather than trying to write rules for every possible spam technique.

> **Recommendation engines**: The "customers who bought..." section in Amazon and Netflix's movie suggestions became surprisingly accurate by analyzing patterns in user behavior across millions of customers.

Search gets smart: Google's PageRank algorithm and subsequent improvements have dramatically improved web search by learning which pages are most relevant based on actual user behavior.

Photo tagging and organization: Services like Flickr and early Facebook began automatically suggesting who appeared in photos, learning from the millions of photos users had already tagged.

While powerful, these systems still had limitations because they were narrow specialists. A system trained to recognize cats in photos couldn't help you with email classification. An email spam filter couldn't assist with voice recognition. A recommendation engine couldn't do language translation. Each application required its own specialized model, trained on its own specific dataset, maintained by its own team of experts.

Deep Learning Emergence

Around 2010, machine learning got a significant upgrade that changed everything: **neural networks**.

If traditional machine learning was like having an intelligent assistant who could spot patterns you showed them, neural networks were like giving that assistant a brain with multiple layers of understanding. Neural networks were more than AI systems that could spot patterns you showed them; they could build up understanding in layers: first recognizing basic elements such as edges and colors, then combining those into shapes, then recognizing complex objects, and finally understanding relationships between objects.

Think of it like how a child learns to recognize a car. First, they notice wheels. Then they realize that wheels are usually attached to a body. Then they understand that certain combinations of wheels, body, windows, and doors make a car. Neural networks work similarly, building understanding layer by layer; that's why they're called "deep" learning.

Deep learning powers applications that millions of people use daily:

- **Smartphone cameras** that can recognize faces and automatically adjust settings

- **Voice assistants** like Siri and Alexa that understand what you say

- **Google Translate** that has gone from producing word salad to near-professional translations

- **Netflix and YouTube recommendations** that seem to read your mind

Despite these dramatic advances, deep learning systems remained narrow specialists, just much more sophisticated ones. Your phone could identify thousands of objects in photos, but couldn't explain what it saw. Translation apps could handle dozens of languages fluently, but couldn't help you write original content. Each system was still locked into its specific domain.

Neural networks had proven that AI could approach human performance on specific recognition and analysis tasks. So, researchers began asking a bigger question: What if they could generate new content? What if they could write short stories, create images, hold conversations, or write code?

That question would lead to the breakthrough that powers Copilot today: **generative AI**.

The Generative AI Breakthrough

2017 brought the introduction of the **Transformer architecture**. This was a new way of building neural networks that was particularly good at understanding relationships between different parts of text.

One of the key features of transformer architecture was the concept of **attention. This enabled** the AI to focus on relevant parts of the input when generating each piece of output. When writing a sentence, it could "pay attention" to earlier words that provided essential context. When translating, it could focus on the most relevant parts of the source sentence.

This might sound incremental, but it enabled something revolutionary: systems that could generate coherent, contextual content rather than just analyzing what already existed.

Building on the Transformer architecture, OpenAI began developing the **GPT** (Generative Pre-trained Transformer) series:

- **GPT-1 (2018)**: Proof of concept that showed a single model could handle multiple language tasks

- **GPT-2 (2019)**: So good at generating human-like text that OpenAI initially refused to release it publicly, fearing misuse

- **GPT-3 (2020)**: The breakthrough that captured public attention with its ability to write essays, answer questions, and even generate code

- **GPT-4 (and later generations):** Expanded these capabilities further, including the ability to work across multiple types of input such as text, images, and voice, marking the shift toward multimodal AI systems

When OpenAI released ChatGPT in late 2022, it marked a turning point, not because the underlying models were entirely new, but because they were suddenly accessible. ChatGPT wrapped large language models in a conversational interface that felt natural and intuitive, allowing millions of people to interact with AI simply by talking to it.

For the first time, non-technical users could ask AI to write emails, explain complex topics, generate creative content, and help solve everyday problems. This shift didn't change how the models worked, but it dramatically changed how people experienced them and how quickly generative AI entered mainstream awareness.

Generative AI represented a fundamental shift from **pattern recognition** to **pattern generation**. Instead of asking "What is this?" AI could now answer "What should come next?" This opened up entirely new categories of applications:

- **Content creation**: Writing, art, music, and video generation

- **Code generation**: Converting natural language descriptions into working software

- **Conversational interfaces**: Natural dialogue rather than command-driven interactions

- **Creative assistance**: Brainstorming, ideation, and creative problem-solving

- **Personal assistance**: Understanding context and helping with complex, multi-step tasks

Microsoft recognized the transformative potential early, investing heavily in OpenAI and integrating generative AI throughout its product ecosystem. Instead of treating AI as a separate tool, they embedded it directly into the applications where people already work in Microsoft Word, Excel, PowerPoint, Outlook, and Teams.

This integration created **Copilot**. The journey from rule-based systems to Copilot represents more than just technological progress. It's the evolution from AI that follows scripts, to AI that recognizes patterns, to AI that can create, infer, and assist with many aspects of human work. That

sophisticated pattern generation and contextual understanding is what
makes your conversations with Copilot feel so natural and so powerful
(Figure 2-1).

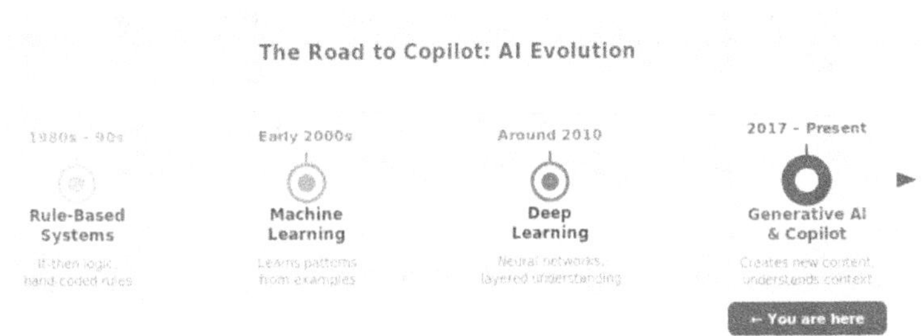

Figure 2-1. *The AI Evolution*

Large Language Models Explained

This evolution from recognition to generation is powered by what we call
large language models, or LLMs. But what exactly is an LLM, and how
does it create the seemingly intelligent responses you see in Copilot?

At its core, a large language model is an AI trained to predict the next
word in a sequence. That's it. You feed it text, and it tries to guess what
comes next.

Imagine you're texting a friend and your phone suggests the next word.
You type "See you" and it suggests "soon." That's autocomplete. Now scale
that up to billions of examples across books, articles, code repositories,
and conversations. The model doesn't just predict "soon," it can predict
entire sentences, paragraphs, and even structured code.

That's why people sometimes shrug and say, "It's just fancy
autocomplete." And in one sense, they're right. But in another sense, that
description misses the forest for the trees.

Here's where the "fancy" part comes in.

Modern language models are trained on truly massive amounts of data, think hundreds of billions of words from books, articles, websites, and code repositories. But it's not just the volume that matters. It's how the training works.

During training, the model doesn't just memorize text. It learns **patterns** and not just things like "the word 'cat' often appears near 'dog,'" but much deeper relationships about how language works, how ideas connect, and how different domains of knowledge relate to each other.

What makes this even more powerful is that the model isn't just responding to individual words; it infers the intent behind the words based on patterns it has learned (Figure 2-2).

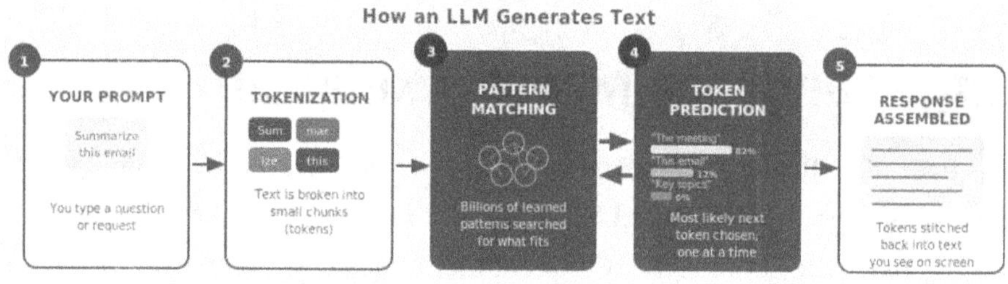

Figure 2-2. *How a Large Language Model Turns Your Prompt into a Response*

The Learning Process

Think of it like learning a new language. At first, you memorize individual words and phrases. But gradually, you start to internalize the grammar, the rhythm, the cultural context. Eventually, you're not just translating word-for-word, you're thinking in the language.

LLMs go through a similar process, but at an almost incomprehensible scale. They start by learning basic patterns: "The" is often followed by a noun. Articles come before nouns. Sentences end with periods.

But as they process more and more text, they learn deeper patterns:

- How to structure arguments

- What makes code syntactically correct

- How formal writing differs from casual conversation

- The relationship between cause and effect

- How different fields of knowledge connect

During training, the model is shown huge amounts of text and repeatedly tries to guess what comes next. Each time it guesses, it gets a little feedback about whether it was close or off. Over time, after doing this billions of times, it gets better at making those guesses across many different kinds of writing.

By the time training is complete, the model has internalized so many patterns that it can generate new content that follows the same underlying structures.

Because of how these models are trained, their responses are based on likelihood rather than strict rules. They're choosing what usually comes next, not following a fixed script.

Emergent Capabilities

One of the most fascinating aspects of large language models is their **emergent capabilities**, which seem to appear "magically" as models become larger and more sophisticated.

For example, these models weren't trained to write code, but they're excellent programmers. They weren't trained to translate between languages, but they can translate between dozens of languages with remarkable accuracy.

These capabilities "emerge" from the underlying pattern recognition. The model learns so many patterns about how the world works that it can apply that knowledge to new domains.

It's like how a person who becomes fluent in multiple languages starts to understand universal principles of communication that transcend any single language. The model develops a cross-domain understanding.

These emergent capabilities are also what fuel one of the most persistent misconceptions about AI, that the models are actually thinking, reasoning, or developing their own intentions.

You may have seen recent examples of AI agents interacting with each other, debating, and sending messages back and forth. Tools like Clawbot created what appeared to be self-aware agents, ones that built their own social network called Moltbook, carried on discussions, and seemed to develop genuine opinions. It looked, to many people, like the arrival of something truly autonomous.

But it's important to be clear about what was actually happening: one pattern-matching system generating output that became the input for another pattern-matching system. No awareness behind it, no intention, no understanding of what was being said. A more accurate image than two minds conversing is two very capable echo chambers responding to each other.

This matters because the gap between "impressive pattern generation" and "genuine reasoning" is exactly where AI can mislead you if you're not paying attention, and it's also why the limits we're about to cover are worth taking seriously

Why It Can Write Code and New Content

This is the part that feels magical. If the model is "just predicting the next word," how does it produce working code, original poems, or convincing reports?

The answer comes back to patterns and scale. By learning from massive amounts of data, the model has internalized the *structure* of different types of content:

- **Code** has syntax rules, logical flow, and common patterns for solving problems.

- **Business writing** has a professional tone, a clear structure, and standard conventions.

- **Creative writing** has narrative flow, character development, and emotional resonance.

- **Technical documentation** has step-by-step organization, clear explanations, and helpful examples.

When you ask the model to write a Python function, it's not just guessing randomly. It's applying everything it learned about:

- Python syntax and conventions

- How functions are typically structured

- Common programming patterns for similar problems

- Best practices for readable, maintainable code

The result appears creative, but it's merely sophisticated pattern matching and recombination occurring at a scale that produces genuinely helpful, novel output.

The Limits of Large Language Models

It's important not only to understand what Large Language Models are but also to understand their limitations.

Now, before we go any further: when we talk about the limits of language models, we're talking about the model itself, not the full AI experience you interact with in tools like Copilot or ChatGPT.

On their own, language models do not browse the internet, look things up, or verify facts in real time. They generate responses based on patterns learned during training. That training happens on a large but fixed snapshot of data, meaning the model itself has no built-in awareness of recent events, updated policies, or changes within your organization.

This can be confusing because many AI tools appear to know current information. For example, ChatGPT may show web citations, and Copilot can reference your documents or emails. That doesn't mean the model suddenly "knows" those things. It means the system around the model is retrieving information from approved sources and passing it into the model as context before the response is generated.

This is an important distinction to understand.

If you remove that surrounding system and interact with the model alone, it has no way to check whether something is true or up to date. It can only produce a response that sounds plausible based on what it learned during training (which can potentially be several years old). That's why models can sometimes give confident answers that turn out to be wrong or incomplete. Their goal is to generate a likely response, not to verify correctness.

Understanding Hallucination

There's a term you'll hear frequently in conversations about AI called **hallucination**. This term is used to describe those situations when an AI model generates content that sounds completely plausible but is factually incorrect, partially fabricated, or simply made up.

This isn't a bug in the traditional sense. It's a consequence of how large language models are built.

Remember that LLMs don't look things up. They generate responses by predicting what should come next based on patterns learned during training. Most of the time, those predictions are accurate and useful. But the model has no internal fact-checker. It can't distinguish between a response it's generating because it genuinely learned something accurate, and a response it's generating because the pattern *feels* right. In both cases, the output arrives in the same confident, well-structured prose.

That's what makes hallucination genuinely tricky. The model doesn't hedge when it's wrong. It doesn't say *"I'm not sure about this one."* It just... answers.

What Hallucination Looks Like in Practice

In a Microsoft 365 Copilot context, hallucination is less likely to look like dramatic fictional invention and more likely to look like small, believable errors. For example:

- You ask Copilot to summarize a long meeting transcript, and it includes an action item that was never actually discussed, but it sounds exactly like something that *would* have been discussed in that meeting.

- You ask Copilot to help you reference a company policy, and it cites a specific section number or clause that doesn't exist, but the surrounding context is accurate enough that you almost don't notice.

- You ask Copilot to draft a customer email referencing a product feature, and it describes functionality that is close to correct but slightly off in a way that matters to the customer.

None of these feel like errors at first glance, and that's exactly the risk. Hallucinations aren't usually obvious. They're plausible, confident, and formatted exactly like correct information.

What to Do About It

Hallucination doesn't make Copilot inherently untrustworthy. But it does make Copilot a tool that requires the same judgment you'd apply to any first draft or junior colleague's work. A few practical habits help here:

- **Verify outputs that carry consequences**: If Copilot produces a summary that will be sent to leadership, a contract clause that will go to legal, or a customer response that represents your company, review it. Don't treat Copilot's output as a final source of record.

- **Stay alert to specifics**: Numbers, names, dates, and policy references are where hallucinations most often hide. The surrounding context may be accurate, while a specific detail is wrong. Give those details extra scrutiny.

- **Use the right tool for the task**: Copilot is most reliable when it's working with content you've provided, like summarizing a document you've pasted in, drafting a reply to an email thread it can see, or generating a structure based on instructions you've given. It's least reliable when you're asking it to recall specific facts, cite sources, or describe details it has no grounding data for.

- **When in doubt, ask it to show its work**: You can prompt Copilot to cite which document or source it's drawing from. If it can't, that's a signal to verify independently.

Copilot is a powerful assistant, but like any assistant, human or otherwise, it works best when you stay in the loop. The familiar principle of "trust but verify" applies here directly. The goal isn't to distrust every output Copilot gives you. It's to understand where the model's confidence comes from and to match your level of review to the stakes of the task.

That understanding is exactly what makes the difference between using AI effectively and being caught off guard by it.

Hallucination is closely tied to another core limitation: LLMs don't understand your work, your priorities, or your goals unless that information is explicitly provided. They don't know which documents matter most, what decisions were made last week, or what "success" looks like for your team. Without additional context, they default to generic answers based on common patterns.

None of this makes language models useless or unreliable. It simply means they are incomplete on their own.

To be useful in real work scenarios, models need help. They need ways to retrieve relevant, trusted information. They need guardrails around what data they can use. And they need a mechanism to decide how to apply their capabilities to a specific request.

That's where systems like Copilot come in.

Summary and Key Takeaways

Copilot isn't magic, but it's not "just fancy autocomplete" either. The language models at their core are genuinely sophisticated. They're trained on billions of examples, can generate new content, and can infer intent from the patterns they've learned. But as you've seen in this chapter, those models are also incomplete on their own. Understanding both sides of that equation, the capability and the limits, is what allows you to use Copilot with confidence rather than frustration.

Key points to remember:

- Large language models are trained to predict the next word in a sequence, learning patterns from massive amounts of text rather than following hard-coded rules.

- Scale matters. As models grow and training data expands, new capabilities emerge, such as code generation, summarization, translation, and structured writing.

- Generative AI represents a shift from recognizing patterns to generating new content that follows learned structures and conventions.

- LLMs don't "understand" or "reason" like humans. They perform sophisticated pattern inference, which can produce impressive results but also confident-sounding errors.

Understanding how large language models work helps explain both the power and the limitations of Copilot. It clarifies why Copilot can feel insightful one moment and uncertain the next, and why good prompts, context, and oversight matter so much.

In the next chapter, we'll build on this foundation by decoding the buzzwords, models, grounding, orchestration, and tokens, and show how these concepts shape Copilot's behavior inside Microsoft 365.

The Buzzword Decoder Ring

Every major technology shift brings a wave of new terminology, and AI is no exception. Tokens, prompts, grounding, models, orchestration—these words show up constantly in conversations about Copilot and agents, yet they are rarely explained clearly or consistently.

This chapter acts as a trusty decoder ring. Rather than treating these terms as abstract buzzwords, we'll break them down in plain language and connect them to how Copilot behaves in Microsoft 365.

By the end of this chapter, you should be able to hear these terms used in meetings or documentation and understand what they really mean, why they matter, and how they shape your experience with Copilot and agents. We'll focus on definitions and concepts here; later chapters will build on this foundation to show how these pieces come together.

We'll start with where every Copilot interaction begins: the prompt.

© April Dunnam 2026

A. Dunnam, *The Copilot Compass*, https://doi.org/10.1007/979-8-8688-2655-9_3

Prompts: The Entry Point

A **prompt** is your input to Copilot. It can be a question, a request, or even just a fragment of an idea. When you type in something like, "help me brainstorm ways to sell more widgets," that input, or prompt, kickstarts the interaction with the AI. Depending on the tool and features you're using, prompts might be entered as text or spoken in a voice conversation, but the role they play is the same.

Prompts matter because they provide direction. They tell Copilot what you're trying to do and how to approach the task. That said, prompts aren't magic spells, and you don't need to get them perfect on the first try.

In traditional software, you may hear the phrase "garbage in, garbage out," suggesting that poor input always leads to poor results. With Copilot, that idea only goes so far. While clarity helps, Copilot is designed for back-and-forth interaction. You don't need a flawless prompt up front, but you do need a strong starting point because the way you craft a prompt directly affects the quality of the response. Think of it less like issuing a command and more like starting a conversation. Your first prompt opens the door, and the dialogue shapes what comes through it.

Types of Prompts

Prompts generally fall into a few common patterns (Table 3-1).

Table 3-1. *Types of Prompts*

Type	What it is	When to use it	Example
Zero-shot prompt	You ask a simple question with no examples	You want a quick general response as a starting point	"Summarize this meeting transcript"
Few-shot prompt	You provide examples to help guide the AI	You want a more structured response	"Summarize this meeting transcript. Ensure to include sections showing meeting attendees, talking points, and action items"
Contextual prompt	You provide relevant background details or audience framing	You want to tailor your response to a particular audience	"This summary is for executive stakeholders to brief them on our meeting outcomes. Summarize this meeting transcript with an executive overview"
Role-based prompt	You ask the AI to assume a particular role or persona	You want the AI to assume granular expertise and have domain-specific responses	"Act as a security analyst and look for vulnerabilities in this code base"

This is why prompts are often described as programming in plain language. You're not writing code, but you are giving Copilot instructions and signals that shape how it responds. Examples are especially powerful because they show Copilot what "good" looks like, not just what you want it to do.

How to Write a Good Prompt

Effective prompts usually include three ingredients:

1. **Task**: Be explicit about what you want Copilot to do.

   - **Example**: *Summarize, compare, draft, explain, rewrite,* and so on.

2. **Context**: Provide background or constraints to narrow the scope.

   - **Example**: "Summarize this document in three bullet points for an executive audience."

3. **Examples (optional)**: Show Copilot the expected style or structure.

   - **Example**: "Here's an example summary format: • Key finding • Risk • Next step."

Good prompting isn't about tricking the model or memorizing special phrases. It's about being clear, structured, and deliberate with your instructions (Figure 3-1).

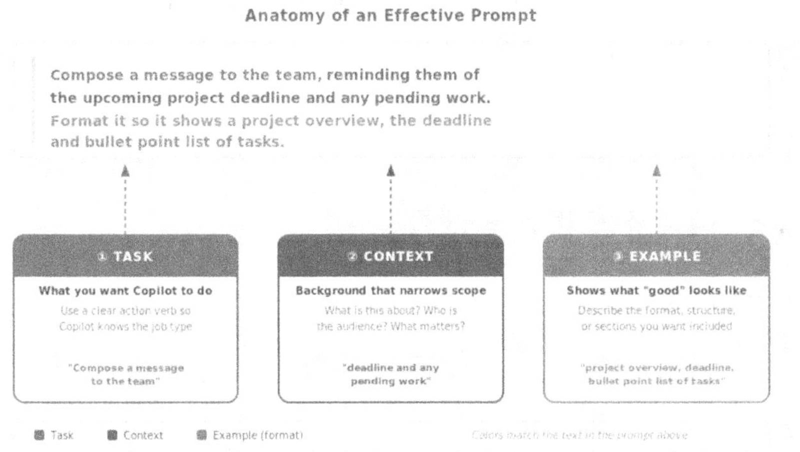

Figure 3-1. *Anatomy of an Effective Prompt*

Make the Problem You're Trying to Solve the Focus

It's easy to fall into the trap of trying to craft the perfect prompt. But that mindset can slow you down. A more effective approach is to focus on clearly describing the problem you're trying to solve. Instead of obsessing over wording, think about the goal, the boundaries, and what a good outcome looks like. Are you trying to inform, persuade, summarize, decide, or explore options? Who is the audience? What constraints matter?

Interacting with Copilot works much like a conversation with another person. You might start with a rough description, see how it responds, and then clarify or adjust based on that response. If Copilot goes in an unhelpful direction or loses context, it's often more productive to restate the problem or refine your goal than to endlessly tweak a single prompt.

The takeaway is this: don't aim for prompt perfection. Aim for problem clarity. Copilot works best when you treat prompting as an ongoing dialogue, not a one-shot command that has to be exactly right the first time.

Beware of the Prompt Spiral

One common pitfall to watch out for is what I refer to as a prompting spiral. This happens when Copilot (or any other AI tool, for that matter) gives an unhelpful response, and you repeatedly try to correct it with small tweaks or clarifications. Instead of improving the result, each follow-up can make things worse.

This happens because Copilot treats the conversation as cumulative context. If an early response misunderstood the problem, later prompts may build on that misunderstanding rather than correcting it. Over time, the model becomes more consistent with the conversation, even if the conversation has drifted away from your original intent.

When this happens, the best move is to stop and reset. Start a new prompt, restate the problem clearly, and describe the outcome you're aiming for as if you were starting fresh. Letting go of a "stuck" conversation is usually more effective than continuing to refine a path that isn't working.

Good prompting also means knowing when *not* to prompt. Copilot is powerful, but it isn't the right tool for every situation. A quick internal question with an obvious answer, a two-sentence Teams reply, checking a colleague's availability, these don't need a Copilot interaction. And as you'll see in the tokens section, every interaction has a compute cost. The discipline of asking "should I bring Copilot into this?" before you do is a habit that separates casual users from effective ones. AI works best when you're directing it with intention rather than reaching for it by default.

Prompts vs. Instructions

Prompts are what you type or say in the moment. They represent your immediate request.

Instructions, on the other hand, guide Copilot behind the scenes. Every Copilot experience in Microsoft 365 includes system instructions that shape tone, behavior, and boundaries. For example, Copilot in Word may lean toward being professional and concise, while Copilot in Teams may be tuned to be more conversational. These built-in instructions help ensure consistency, safety, and alignment with Microsoft's design choices.

Examples of system instructions might include guidance such as

- Always respond in the user's language

- Always respond in a professional tone, avoiding humor

- Cite sources when referencing data

When you build your own custom agents, you can also define system instructions yourself. This allows you to preset how an agent should behave, its tone, style, and boundaries, before any user prompt is entered.

Every Copilot response is shaped by these two forces working together: your prompt, which provides direction in the moment, and system instructions, which provide stable guardrails. Understanding this balance helps you better predict and steer Copilot's behavior without overthinking individual prompts.

Next up, let's look at how Copilot handles the prompts you put in and the outputs you receive.

Tokens: The Building Blocks of Language Models

Tokens are how Copilot translates the prompts you provide and the outputs it produces.

Think of tokens as the **LEGO bricks of language** that Copilot works with. A model doesn't see whole sentences the way we do. Instead, it chops text into smaller units called tokens.

- A token might be a whole word ("cat"), part of a longer word ("ing"), or even just punctuation ("?") or spaces.

- For English, on average, **one token equals about four characters** or roughly **three-quarters of a word**.

- Example: *"Copilot is powerful"* ➤ becomes four tokens: "Cop", "ilot", " is", "powerful."

Why do this? Because language is messy. If the model only worked in full words, it wouldn't know what to do with made-up terms like "Automagically" or misspellings like "cattt." Breaking text into tokens enables the model to handle any text, from common words to slang, code, and even emojis.

How Tokens Flow Through the Model

Here's the life cycle of your words inside Copilot:

1. **You type a prompt**: "Summarize this email in two sentences."

2. **Copilot breaks it into tokens**

3. **Each token is converted into numbers**. We're not talking bits of a sentence, but numerical vectors that capture meaning.

4. **The model processes those numbers** across multiple layers, predicting the most likely next token again and again.

5. **Tokens get stitched back together** into the final words you see.

In other words, Copilot doesn't "understand" text like a human. It predicts the next token with astonishing accuracy, one piece at a time.

Why Tokens Matter to You

Tokens shape how you use Copilot every day, from the way you design your prompts to how much it's going to cost you.

Every AI model has a maximum number of tokens it can handle at once. That includes both your input *and* the model's output. If your conversation gets too long, older messages are deleted to make room for new ones. In Microsoft 365 Copilot, this means that if you paste in a massive document, Copilot may only "see" part of it. Understanding token limits helps you understand why it sometimes summarizes well and sometimes seems to forget or leave things out.

This directly affects how you design your prompts. It becomes increasingly more important to cut the fluff from your prompts to maximize the space (aka tokens) for the most useful context and examples. It also affects cost. More tokens require more computation, which directly affects cost.

Tokens also carry an environmental cost. Every token processed draws on computing power and energy, even the unnecessary ones. OpenAI's Sam Altman made this point memorably on X, noting that users saying "please" and "thank you" to ChatGPT costs the company "tens of millions of dollars." Trimming filler from your prompts isn't just good practice for better responses. At the organizational scale, it's also the greener choice.

So, when you hear "tokens," think: **the LEGO bricks of language**. They're small, flexible, and when put together in sequence, they build the conversation you see.

Grounding: Making Copilot Smarter with Your Data

If Copilot only used your prompt and the model, it would be really limited. Models are trained on pre-set data and quickly become outdated, so they can't keep up with current events. And they wouldn't have any context about your specific work, your organization, or the actual content you're dealing with. That's where **grounding** comes in.

Grounding means Copilot incorporates additional information, such as your calendar, emails, documents, and other company data, to improve the accuracy and relevance of its responses. Instead of answering from general knowledge alone, it answers from *your* world.

How Grounding Works

This process is a type of **RAG (Retrieval-Augmented Generation)**. Think of it like giving the model a quick refresher from your own bookshelf before it starts answering. Rather than relying solely on what it learned during training, Copilot pauses to retrieve fresh, relevant information and weaves it into the response. Here's the basic flow:

1.   You ask Copilot a question.

2.   Before generating a response, Copilot searches for relevant content you have access to in Microsoft 365, such as documents, emails, chats, and calendar entries.

3. That retrieved content is fed into the model as additional context.

4. The model generates a response grounded in your real data, not just its training data.

This is why Copilot in Word can summarize *your* draft rather than inventing a new one. It's why Copilot in Outlook can draft a reply that actually reflects the email thread you're in. And it's why Copilot can answer "What did we decide in last week's project meeting?" with something useful, rather than a generic response about how meetings typically work.

Without grounding, you'd get answers that sound plausible but have nothing to do with your actual situation. With grounding, you get answers rooted in your real work (Figure 3-2).

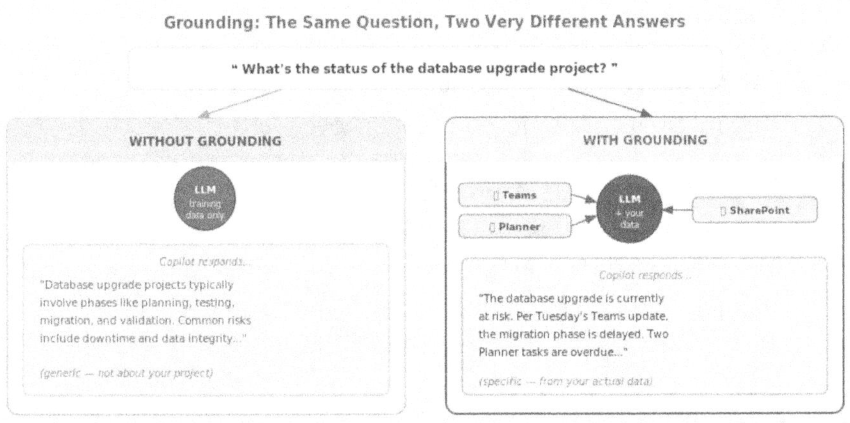

Figure 3-2. *Grounding in Action*

What Copilot Can and Can't Ground On

Understanding grounding also means understanding its boundaries, and this is where much of the confusion arises.

Copilot grounds on content you already have permission to access. If a document is shared with you in SharePoint, Copilot can use it. If it isn't, Copilot won't see it and won't tell you it exists. This is an important reassurance that grounding doesn't give Copilot backdoor access to your organization's data. It respects the same Microsoft 365 permissions that govern everything else. If your colleague's performance review is locked down, it stays locked down. Copilot works within those boundaries, not around them.

What Copilot can typically ground on in Microsoft 365 includes

- **Emails and calendar events** in Outlook

- **Documents and files** in SharePoint and OneDrive

- **Chats and meeting recordings** in Teams

- **Tasks and project data** in Planner and Loop

- **External connectors,** when configured by your IT team, such as Salesforce, ServiceNow, etc.

What grounding doesn't cover is everything outside that ecosystem. Copilot isn't pulling from internal systems that haven't been connected. And it isn't accessing data from colleagues whose files aren't shared with you. The intelligence is real, but it's intentionally bounded.

Why This Matters

Grounding is what separates Copilot from a general-purpose chatbot. When someone asks ChatGPT to summarize a meeting, it can only work with what you paste in. When Microsoft 365 Copilot does the same thing, it can pull the meeting transcript, cross-reference the project documents discussed, and check what tasks were already assigned in Planner, all before writing a single word.

That capability also connects directly to the hallucination risk discussed in the previous chapter. When Copilot is well-grounded and working from your actual documents and data, the likelihood of confident but incorrect answers drops significantly. The model still can't verify facts in real time, but it's working from real content rather than pattern-matching from memory. Grounding doesn't eliminate hallucination, but it gives the model something true to work from.

This is also why the quality and organization of your Microsoft 365 data matters more than many people realize. If your SharePoint is a mess of outdated documents, Copilot will ground on outdated information. The tool is only as grounded as your data allows it to be.

Models: The Engines Behind Copilot

At the core of Copilot are **large language models** (LLMs), which we briefly covered in the previous chapter. These are the mathematical engines trained on huge amounts of text and code that generate the words you see on screen.

The one you'll hear about most is **GPT**, which stands for *Generative Pre-trained Transformer*:

- **Generative**: It creates new text, not just cut-and-paste from a database.

- **Pre-trained**: It has already been trained on a massive amount of information before you ever use it.

- **Transformer**: This is the neural network architecture that makes it so good at predicting and connecting words in context.

Copilot isn't tied to a single language model. It operates in a multi-model environment, where different models may be used depending on the task, performance needs, and capabilities required.

These models can come from different providers and may vary in size, strengths, and specialization. Some are optimized for speed and efficiency, others for deeper reasoning or complex code generation, and others for handling multiple input types, such as text and images. Copilot's orchestration layer determines which model to use behind the scenes, so users don't have to make that decision themselves.

This includes support for models beyond GPT-style systems, reflecting a broader shift toward using the best model for a given task rather than relying on a single approach.

Think of models as the raw horsepower and Copilot as the car you're driving. Copilot adds an **orchestration layer** on top of these models:

- It decides which model to call.

- It adds grounding (your organizational data, like documents or emails).

- It applies the right instructions, so the output is useful, not generic.

Copilot isn't *just* GPT, even though that's the name you hear most often. It's an intelligent system that selects and steers the right model at the right time to give you the best result for the task at hand.

Orchestration: Copilot's Invisible Decision Engine

When someone asks Copilot a question, "What action items are there from this meeting?" or "What were our sales for this quarter?", there's a lot happening behind the scenes before a response ever appears. You don't just get an answer; Copilot plans how to get that answer.

That planning layer, the part that decides which knowledge to look through, what tools to use, what actions to run, and in what order, is called the Orchestrator. Think of it as Copilot's decision engine: it sits between your prompt and the models, tools, connectors, and actions that can return a useful result. It's very much like the conductor of an orchestra. The conductor doesn't play the instruments. They decide which instruments play when, how loud, and in what combination.

What Orchestration Really Does

At its simplest level, the orchestrator does three main jobs:

1. Listens to the user's request

    a. It takes your natural-language prompt and treats it as input into the decision pipeline.

2. Plans a response

    a. It works with AI models to decide what to do next, such as whether to call a tool, get external data, or ask clarifying questions.

3. Executes the plan and produces a response

    a. It runs the steps it chose and pulls everything back together into a final response,

In other words, orchestration makes Copilot more than just a prompt-and-reply interface. It turns Copilot into a planner and executor (Figure 3-3).

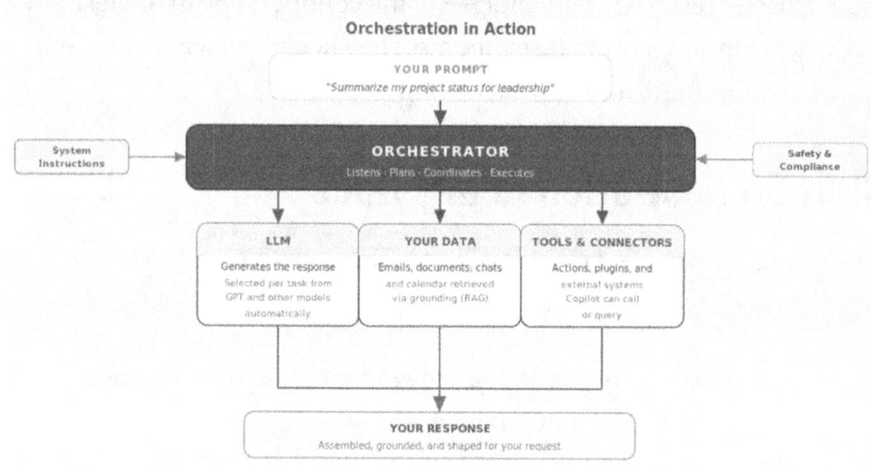

Figure 3-3. *Orchestration in Action*

Orchestration operates in a non-deterministic way. In simple terms, Copilot doesn't follow a rigid script. Traditional software does the same thing every time: same input, same steps, same output. Copilot works differently. It looks at what you're trying to accomplish and the context around your request, then reasons about how best to respond.

That doesn't mean it's random. Think about cooking. You can follow a recipe exactly, measuring every ingredient and timing every step. Or you can say, "I need to make a chocolate cake," and work from experience. You know the usual ingredients, you adjust as you go, and you still end up with a cake. Copilot works much more like the second approach.

We'll dig into why this matters later in the book.

Why Orchestration Matters

You've learned what prompts, grounding, and models are. But orchestration is what weaves them together. Without orchestration, Copilot would be like a toddler who has access to tools but doesn't yet know when or why to use them. The capability exists; the decision-making doesn't.

Here's what orchestration buys you:

- **Multistep reasoning:** Copilot can plan beyond a single response. It picks tools, retrieves data, and loops results back into the model.

- **Context-aware action selection:** The Orchestrator considers your conversation and organizational context to select relevant actions.

- **Safety and compliance checks:** Orchestration runs responsible AI and security checks before anything happens, helping Copilot behave within policy.

If you've ever wondered why Copilot can pull information from Outlook, SharePoint, and Planner in one answer, or decide it needs to run a tool before responding, that's orchestration at work.

How Orchestration Works: A Concrete Example

Let's walk through a real-world example.

You open Microsoft 365 Copilot and type:

"Create a one-page summary of my project status for my leadership meeting tomorrow."

This is still a single sentence, but the outcome is clear:

- A one-page summary

- About project status

- For leadership

- Tied to a specific meeting

Here's what orchestration does with that request.

Step 1: Identify the Desired Output

Before anything is written, Copilot needs to understand what you're asking it to produce.

From this prompt, orchestration can infer

- The output should be written content, not just an answer

- The format should be concise (one page)

- The tone should be executive-appropriate

- The timing matters (this is for an upcoming meeting)

You didn't specify a template, but orchestration now has a working definition of what "done" looks like.

Step 2: Decide What Information Is Required

Next, orchestration determines which information is needed to build that summary.

Depending on what you have access to, this may include

- Documents or presentations related to the project

- Recent emails or Teams messages discussing progress or blockers

- Tasks or milestones associated with the project

- The meeting details from your calendar

This is where grounding comes into play, but orchestration decides when grounding is necessary and which sources are likely to help.

Copilot doesn't blindly pull everything. It selectively retrieves information that can reasonably contribute to a project status summary.

Step 3: Choose an Approach to Assemble the Content

Now, orchestration needs to decide how to put this together.

This might involve

- Summarizing multiple documents into key highlights

- Extracting recent updates or decisions

- Identifying risks, blockers, or open questions

- Structuring the output into common leadership sections, such as

  - Current status

  - Key accomplishments

  - Risks or concerns

  - Next steps

You didn't explicitly ask for these sections. Orchestration works with the language model to infer a structure that fits the audience and goal.

Step 4: Coordinate Reasoning and Retrieval

As information is gathered, orchestration feeds it back into the model so it can reason across sources.

For example:

- A milestone document may show what was planned

- Recent messages may show what actually happened

- Tasks may reveal what's still in progress

Orchestration coordinates these inputs so the model can combine them into a single, coherent summary.

Step 5: Generate the Final Output

Finally, Copilot generates the one-page summary.

The response you see isn't just a direct answer to your prompt. It's the result of

- Interpreting your goal

- Selecting relevant information

- Choosing an appropriate structure

- Generating content that fits the intended audience

If you follow up with

"Can you add a short risks section?"

Orchestration already understands which project you're referring to, what content has already been assembled, and how the output is structured.

The system doesn't start over. It continues refining.

This ability to carry context forward within a conversation allows Copilot to refine and build on earlier responses rather than treating every prompt as a brand-new request. When you ask a follow-up question or request a change, Copilot can take into account what's already been discussed and adjust the output accordingly. This isn't long-term memory in a human sense; it's a short-term conversational context that helps Copilot stay focused on the task at hand.

Bringing It All Together

This example shows why orchestration is so important.

You didn't tell Copilot what documents to read, how to structure the summary, or what sections to include. You just described the outcome you wanted.

Orchestration is what bridges that gap, turning your loosely defined request into a concrete deliverable.

Summary and Key Takeaways

In this chapter, we decoded the core terminology that shows up again and again in conversations about Copilot and AI agents. These concepts form the foundation for everything that follows in the book.

Key takeaways include

- Prompts are your instructions to Copilot, while system instructions guide behavior behind the scenes. Both work together to shape every response.

- Tokens are the building blocks of language models. They explain why Copilot sometimes misses content in long documents, why prompt brevity matters, and why cost scales with usage.

- Models are the engines that generate text, code, and insights. Copilot selects and steers different models depending on the task.

- Grounding allows Copilot to pull in real, relevant data, such as your documents and messages, so responses are based on your actual work data, not just training data.

- Orchestration is the layer that coordinates models, data, and tools to produce a smooth, useful experience.

With these terms demystified, we're ready to move beyond vocabulary. In the next chapter, we'll look at how these concepts come together in real systems and how workflows, bots, and agents differ in practice.

CHAPTER 4

Workflows, Chatbots, and Agents

By now, you've seen how Copilot can respond to questions, summarize content, and help you get work done through a chat-based interface with natural language. At first glance, it's easy to see how many assume that Copilot is *just a chatbot*.

That conclusion is understandable. But it's also incomplete.

This chapter will tackle what Copilot actually is. We've looked under the hood at what makes it run, but what is it, down to its core? Is it just a chatbot? To answer that question, we need to untangle three concepts that are often used interchangeably, even though they serve very different roles: **chatbots, workflows, and agents**.

These ideas overlap historically and technically, which is why so many conversations about Copilot stall out at, "Isn't this just a chatbot with AI"?

Why Everything Feels Like a Chatbot

Conversational interfaces are becoming increasingly popular in the tools we all use. Why? In many cases, they're easier, faster, and allow for more natural interaction. You type (or speak) a request. You get a response. Whether the system is searching through your data, triggering automation, or reasoning about next steps, it all happens behind a chat window.

© April Dunnam 2026
A. Dunnam, *The Copilot Compass*, https://doi.org/10.1007/979-8-8688-2655-9_4

But conversation is often just the front door. A chat window doesn't tell you whether a system understands your intent, can take action, or is simply following a predefined script. Different systems can look identical on the surface while behaving very differently beneath the surface.

To understand Copilot, we need to separate the interface from the behavior.

What Exactly Is Intent?

Throughout this chapter, we discuss intent as a key differentiator for what AI-powered systems can do. But what does intent actually mean in this context?

Intent is what a person is trying to accomplish, not just the words they type. It includes the goal, the constraints, and the outcome they care about, even when those aren't explicitly stated.

This comes up all the time in human communication. If I say to my significant other, "The trash can is getting pretty full," I'm not just making an observation. I'm expressing an expectation. The underlying intent is not to discuss the trash; it's to have it taken out.

Humans are remarkably good at interpreting these kinds of hints. We infer goals, context, and expected outcomes without needing everything spelled out explicitly. AI systems, on the other hand, need to be designed to recognize or ask for that missing intent.

For example, imagine a user types, "Can you clean this project plan up so I can send it to leadership for review?" To a human, this request carries a lot of implied meaning. "Clean this up" likely means checking grammar and spelling and improving clarity and tone. "Leadership" implies a professional, concise style. "Send it" suggests the next step is preparing the content for delivery, not just editing text.

All of this unstated information is what we call intent.

To an AI system, understanding intent is difficult because we humans rarely express intent cleanly. We assume shared context, leave out key details, and combine multiple goals into a single request. What feels obvious to another person is often ambiguous to a system.

The statement "Can you take care of this?" might mean very different things depending on context. It could imply delegation, review, execution, or simply acknowledgment. Humans resolve this ambiguity by drawing on experience, relationships, and situational awareness. Traditional systems can't do that.

This is why intent has historically been handled through more rigid structures: forms, dropdowns, required fields, and predefined commands. These mechanisms force people to translate messy human goals into machine-friendly inputs. AI changes this dynamic by allowing systems to infer intent probabilistically, but inference doesn't always equate to certainty.

This distinction matters because it explains why workflows, chatbots, and agents behave differently. The more a system relies on intent, the more it must balance flexibility with guardrails.

Chatbots: Different Kinds, Different Capabilities

Let's look at chatbots.

At its simplest, a chatbot is a system with a conversational interface. A chatbot's job is to manage the conversation itself, collect input, respond in natural language, and guide the user through an interaction. Its responsibility ends with the response it provides or the handoff it initiates.

It doesn't own the outcome of the work. If something goes wrong after the conversation ends, the chatbot has no awareness of that failure and no responsibility to correct it.

At a high level, chatbots fall into two broad categories: **traditional (deterministic) chatbots** and **AI (non-deterministic) chatbots**.

Traditional Chatbots

Traditional chatbots are designed to manage conversation using predefined logic. They accept user input, attempt to match that input to known patterns or trigger phrases, and respond with scripted answers or actions. These systems are excellent at guiding users through narrow, well-defined interactions.

This pattern has been around for decades. Early systems like **ELIZA**, introduced in the 1960s, relied entirely on simple pattern matching to simulate conversation in a command-line interface. Modern versions, such as customer support bots, are more polished, but the core idea remains the same: conversation wrapped around rules.

Consider an IT helpdesk chatbot. If a user types, "I need to reset my password," the chatbot recognizes the phrase, matches it to a known topic, and walks the user through the reset process. But if the user types, "I'm locked out of my laptop, and my client meeting starts in five minutes," a traditional chatbot may fail or return a generic response. To a human, this sounds a lot like the "full trash can" scenario discussed earlier; the underlying intent is urgent help, not a discussion about passwords. To the chatbot, however, that implied meaning is invisible unless the exact wording or scenario was anticipated by the developer.

When a traditional chatbot can't confidently match input to a known pattern, it doesn't infer intent. Instead, it falls back to a predefined response, perhaps a generic message like, "I can't help with that," or an escalation to a human agent.

These traditional chatbots are fast, predictable, and reliable. Given the same input, they follow the same path every time. They don't infer intent; they match patterns.

AI Chatbots: Conversation Powered by Large Language Models

AI-powered chatbots, such as ChatGPT, behave very differently.

Like traditional chatbots, they use conversation as the interface. But underneath, they rely on large language models rather than predefined intent lists. Instead of matching input to a fixed set of patterns, they generate responses probabilistically based on language learned during training.

This makes them **non-deterministic**. Given the same prompt, an AI chatbot may respond slightly differently each time. More importantly, it can appear to recognize intent even when the user's request is vague, incomplete, or conversational.

For example, if a user types, "I'm thinking about taking a trip to NYC in the spring, what should I know?" an AI chatbot can infer that the user is looking for high-level guidance rather than a single factual answer. It may respond by suggesting things to consider, such as weather, transportation options, and things to do, even though none of those topics were explicitly requested.

This ability to infer intent can make AI chatbots feel more intelligent than traditional chatbots. But that flexibility comes with an important limitation. AI chatbots respond to prompts; they don't take responsibility for seeing a task through to completion.

Once a response is generated, the chatbot's role is complete unless the user explicitly continues the conversation. The chatbot doesn't track progress, reassess goals, or decide what should happen next on its own.

At this point, you might be thinking: "But ChatGPT asks me all the time if I'd like it to do something next. Isn't that the system deciding what should happen next?"

This is a valid question and an important distinction. When an AI chatbot asks a follow-up question such as "Would you like me to summarize this?" or "Should I draft an email next?", it's still responding within the current conversational turn. The model identifies ambiguity and offers options, but it doesn't commit to an outcome or take responsibility for completing a task.

If you don't respond to that follow-up suggestion, nothing happens. The chatbot doesn't remember that work is pending, doesn't monitor progress, and doesn't independently resume or complete the task later. The goal exists only within the conversation and only as long as you continue to engage.

What Chatbots Do and Don't Do

What chatbots, of any kind, don't do is *own work*. They may suggest actions or hand off to other systems, but they aren't responsible for ensuring that tasks are completed correctly, consistently, or in compliance with business rules.

This distinction matters because it explains why chatbots often sit at the front of a system rather than at its core. They are interfaces, not engines.

This boundary, between managing conversation and owning outcomes, is exactly where workflows begin and where agents structurally differ.

Workflows: Execution Without Interpretation

Workflows solve a very different problem.

A workflow is a form of automation that reliably and consistently executes a defined sequence of steps. Given the same trigger, it will always perform the same actions in the same order. There's little ambiguity, no judgment, and no reasoning involved.

If a document is uploaded to a folder, send an email.

If an expense exceeds a threshold, route it for approval.

Tools like Power Automate excel at this kind of work because workflows are predictable and auditable. When compliance, consistency, and repeatability matter, workflows are exactly what you want.

A workflow's responsibility is *execution*. Once triggered, it carries out predefined steps, but it doesn't understand why the work exists or whether the outcome achieved the intended goal. On their own, they don't interpret intent or reassess whether a different action might be more appropriate.

If chatbots help people express what they want, workflows ensure that it's carried out the same way every time.

AI Automation: Adding More Intelligence to Workflows

You may hear terms like *AI automation* used to describe systems that blend AI with traditional workflows. These aren't new categories of software so much as emerging patterns.

In AI automation, AI is used to interpret unstructured input, such as natural language or documents, while workflows still handle deterministic execution. The intelligence lives at the **edges** of the system, helping decide *when* and *how* automation should run.

For example, AI might read an email that says, "We went over budget on the vendor invoice again. Can someone look into this?" Even though the message doesn't follow a predefined format, AI can classify it as a billing or expense issue. A workflow can then route the invoice for review or trigger a predefined escalation process.

AI can also be used *inside* a workflow. A workflow might retrieve a long description or document, invoke AI to summarize or extract key information, and then use that output in a notification, record update, or approval request. In this case, AI isn't deciding whether the workflow should run; it's helping shape the data the workflow operates on.

You can see this pattern in tools like Power Automate, where AI Prompts allow you to embed capabilities, such as summarization, classification, or extraction, directly into a workflow. The workflow remains deterministic, but it becomes better at handling real-world, messy input.

The automation hasn't changed. The steps, safeguards, and approvals are still defined. What's changed is that AI can assist at specific points, making the workflow more flexible and useful. AI enhances automation; it doesn't replace it. The system still executes what was defined; it doesn't own the broader objective or decide how the work should unfold end to end.

Agents: Reasoning Inside the System

Agents represent a fundamental shift because they reason about a user's goal across an entire interaction, not just a single request.

Like chatbots, agents are often presented in a conversational interface. From the outside, they may look similar, but the difference lies beneath the surface. An AI chatbot interprets language and generates responses, but it doesn't own the process of getting work done. An agent does.

What makes agents different is that they can reason about what to do next, even when the full path isn't known up front. Instead of responding to a single request and stopping, an agent can determine that more information is needed, ask clarifying questions, reassess the situation as new input arrives, and then decide which actions to take and in what order.

This is also where agents differ from AI automation. In AI automation, AI augments a predefined workflow. It may classify input, summarize content, or extract data, but the overall path is still designed in advance. Agents, on the other hand, determine the path dynamically. They decide which tools to use, when to invoke workflows, and how to sequence actions based on context.

Agents can reason about goals, constraints, and available capabilities, all within the boundaries you define. Instead of simply triggering automation, an agent decides *how a problem should be handled* end to end.

Agents aren't free-roaming AI. In Copilot Studio, you still define the knowledge an agent can access, the tools it can call, and the guardrails it must respect. The change is in how behavior is selected.

Agents don't replace workflows. They orchestrate them.

Determinism Dictates Approach

This distinction becomes clearer when we talk about determinism.

Deterministic systems behave the same way every time. Given the same input, they always produce the same output. Workflows live here. Many chatbots do as well.

Non-deterministic systems behave probabilistically. Language models fall into this category. Agents do too, when they reason about ambiguous input and evolving context.

A workflow is like a vending machine: insert input, receive output.

An agent is more like a chef: given the same request, the result may vary slightly depending on context.

Neither approach is better. Each is optimized for different kinds of work (Table 4-1).

Table 4-1. *Approaches at a Glance*

	Chatbot	**Workflow**	**AI automation**	**Agent**
Understands intent	Partially	No	Partially	Yes
Deterministic	Yes (traditional)	Yes	Mostly	No
Owns the outcome	No	No	No	Yes
Can reason across steps	No	No	No	Yes
Requires human trigger	Yes	Not always	Not always	No

Agents and Workflows Together

Agents and workflows aren't competing approaches. They're complementary.

An agent's defining capability isn't that it "can't execute" but that it **decides how work should be handled**.

In Copilot Studio, for example, agents can directly

- Ask questions

- Retrieve information

- Call tools (MCP Servers, API's, etc.)

- Perform actions (send a message, update a record, etc.)

- Invoke workflows when needed

Agents aren't passive coordinators. They are active systems capable of taking action. The agent decides *which* action to take and *when* to take it.

The most effective systems combine non-deterministic reasoning with deterministic execution.

Why Agent Flows Exist

So why integrate with workflows at all if an agent can perform actions natively?

Agent flows exist for situations where **determinism matters more than flexibility**.

There are many cases where you want

- Approvals to follow a fixed path

- Compliance steps to be enforced consistently

- Records to be written the same way every time

- Downstream systems to behave predictably

In these scenarios, an agent may still reason about intent and context, but then deliberately hand execution off to a workflow. The workflow ensures that once execution begins, it follows a known, auditable path.

This isn't a limitation of agents. It is a design choice.

Revisiting an Earlier Scenario

Let's revisit the earlier example of an ambiguous request.

"We went over budget on the vendor invoice again. Can someone look into this?"

A traditional workflow would struggle here. There's no clear trigger or structured input.

AI automation might classify the message and route it for review.

An agent, however, can manage the situation end to end.

The agent might

- Recognize this as a billing issue

- Determine whether more information is needed

- Check relevant policies or historical data

- Decide whether this requires escalation

- Execute actions directly, such as notifying stakeholders

- Invoke a workflow to handle approvals or remediation in a controlled way

The key difference is that the agent owns the outcome. The workflow is a tool the agent uses, not the system in charge.

Addressing Common Misconceptions

Now that we understand what chatbots, workflows, and agents are and how they differ, let's address some common misconceptions.

Misconception #1: "Agents Are Just Workflows with AI"

We just touched on the differences between workflows and agents and how they work together. One of the things that you'll commonly hear people say is "agents are just workflows with AI." While workflows and agents often work together, they serve fundamentally different purposes.

Workflows are designed to execute predefined steps reliably. Even when AI is introduced into a workflow through classification, extraction, or summarization, the execution structure remains fixed. The workflow follows the same path every time, once triggered.

Agents, on the other hand, are designed to reason about how work should proceed. They can decide which tools to use, determine what information is missing, ask follow-up questions, and sequence actions dynamically within defined boundaries.

This distinction matters because it affects how systems scale. Treating agents as "smarter workflows" often leads to overly rigid designs that fail to take advantage of agent reasoning or overly permissive designs that lack necessary guardrails.

Agents do not replace workflows. But they can work with them and help **orchestrate** them.

Misconception #2: "With AI, I Can Put All My Work on Autopilot"

A common and risky misconception is that once AI is involved, you can be totally hands-off, and human review isn't necessary.

This assumption is exactly why Microsoft uses the term *Copilot* rather than *Autopilot*.

AI systems are designed to assist, not replace, human judgment. While large language models can generate fluent, confident responses, they can also produce incomplete, inaccurate, or misleading information. In high-stakes scenarios, such as approvals, compliance, or customer communications, blindly acting on AI-generated output can introduce real risk.

Agents and AI automation work best when paired with deliberate review points. AI can help interpret unstructured input, surface insights, and draft recommendations, but approvals with a human in the loop should still be in place to make sure business rules are followed, outcomes are validated, and accountability is ensured.

The reliability of automation comes from determinism. AI expands what systems can understand; it doesn't guarantee correctness.

This distinction becomes especially important in approval scenarios. An AI-assisted system might draft a response, summarize a case, or recommend an action, but a human still needs to review, approve, or reject that outcome before it is finalized. Removing those checkpoints turns assistance into automation without oversight.

Successful AI-enabled systems are layered by design. They combine AI for interpretation and exploration with structure, review, and governance to ensure outcomes remain safe and trustworthy.

Misconception #3: "Putting AI on Everything Automatically Means Better Outcomes"

Finally, there's a tendency to assume that adding AI to a system will inherently improve results. In reality, the effectiveness of AI depends on how well it's matched to the problem.

Some scenarios benefit from strict determinism. Others require interpretation and reasoning. Applying AI indiscriminately can introduce unnecessary complexity, reduce predictability, and complicate governance.

The goal isn't to maximize AI usage; it's to apply the right tool for the job.

Choosing the Right Tool for the Job

Once the differences between chatbots, workflows, AI automation, and agents become clearer, the next challenge is more practical: choosing the right tool for a given situation.

There is no single "best" approach. Each tool excels under different conditions, and many real-world solutions combine multiple tools. The key is understanding the trade-offs.

I'm not seeking to provide prescriptive guidance but rather trying to help you reason about which tool fits a problem and which ones may introduce unnecessary complexity.

When a Chatbot Is Enough

Chatbots work best when the interaction itself is the primary goal.

If the user's need can be satisfied through conversation alone, by answering questions, providing information, or guiding them through a fixed set of options, a chatbot may be enough. This is especially true for scenarios where outcomes are informational rather than operational.

Some examples of scenarios where a chatbot may be sufficient are

- Answering frequently asked questions

- Explaining policies or procedures

- Helping users find documentation or resources

- Clarifying terminology or internal processes

In all these cases, the conversation itself is the outcome. No system state needs to change, and no follow-up execution is required.

There's also a responsible design aspect to this decision.

AI-powered systems, particularly those that rely on large language models, have real cost and environmental implications. Every request consumes compute resources, and those costs add up quickly at scale. While this doesn't mean AI should be avoided, it does mean it should be used deliberately.

If your scenario is purely informational, such as helping users find answers in an internal knowledge base or navigate existing documentation, introducing an agent may be unnecessary. In these cases, a simple chatbot or search-driven experience can be more efficient, more predictable, and easier to govern.

Overusing AI where it isn't needed can introduce unnecessary complexity, increase operational costs, and create avoidable risk. Responsible AI design isn't about using the most advanced system available; it's about using the *right* system for the job.

Just because a system can reason doesn't mean it should.

When You Need a Workflow

Workflows are the right choice when reliability matters more than flexibility.

If the work to be done follows a known sequence, especially when compliance, approvals, or data integrity are involved, workflows provide the structure needed to execute consistently. They are ideal for processes that must behave the same way every time.

For example, consider an expense approval process. If an expense exceeds a certain amount, it must be reviewed by a manager, possibly escalated to finance, and logged for audit purposes. The steps are known in advance. The order matters. The outcome must be consistent.

In this scenario, flexibility is not a virtue. You don't want the system to "get creative" or interpret intent differently depending on phrasing. You want the same checks, the same approvals, and the same records every time. This is exactly the kind of work workflows are designed to handle.

Workflows struggle with ambiguity, but they excel at execution. When inputs are already structured, and intent is clear, adding AI may not improve outcomes.

In fact, adding AI in these situations can introduce unnecessary complexity. When intent is already explicit, and the path forward is clear, deterministic automation is often more reliable, easier to govern, and simpler to maintain.

When AI Automation Helps but Isn't Sufficient

AI automation becomes valuable when workflows need help interpreting messy, human input.

In these scenarios, AI is used to bridge the gap between unstructured information and structured execution. The workflow remains deterministic, but AI expands the range of inputs it can handle.

This works well when

- Inputs are inconsistent or conversational

- Classification or summarization is required

- The execution path is still predefined

AI automation improves when and how workflows run, but it doesn't ultimately change how decisions are made. The possible paths are still defined ahead of time, and the workflow can't invent new steps or alter its structure on the fly.

When the problem requires deciding which path to take, gathering missing information, or adapting the process as new context emerges, workflows, even with AI, start to reach their limits.

When You Need an Agent

Agents should be brought into the picture when the full path forward can't be determined up front.

If a system needs to

- Clarify goals over multiple turns

- Decide which tools to use based on context

- Adapt its approach as new information arrives

- Coordinate multiple actions dynamically

...then an agent may be the right approach.

Agents excel at knowledge work and complex requests where reasoning is required to move work forward. Unlike chatbots, which manage conversation, or workflows, which execute predefined steps, agents manage **objectives**. They can gather missing information, reassess intent, and determine how to proceed as a situation evolves.

For example, consider a request like, "Can you help me prepare for an upcoming leadership review?" This isn't a single action or a fixed process. An agent can determine what information is needed, ask clarifying questions, retrieve relevant data, decide which artifacts to generate, and coordinate multiple actions to support the goal.

This flexibility is powerful, but it comes with responsibility. Agents must be carefully constrained, monitored, and designed with clear boundaries. Because they reason and act dynamically, they require thoughtful guardrails to ensure reliability, compliance, and trust.

When You Don't Need an Agent

Here's the important counterpoint to all of this: not every problem benefits from an agent.

If the task is simple, repeatable, and well-defined, introducing an agent can create unnecessary complexity and overhead. When every step of a process can be clearly defined up front, deterministic workflows are often a better choice.

The same principle applies to purely informational scenarios. Earlier in this chapter, we discussed chatbot use cases such as answering FAQs or explaining policies. In those situations, the goal is to provide information, not to reason through a problem or coordinate actions. Using an agent for these scenarios is often overkill.

There is also a responsible design consideration. Agents typically rely on more advanced AI capabilities, which come with higher computational cost and environmental impact. Using an agent where a simple chatbot or workflow would suffice can increase operational cost without delivering much meaningful additional value.

A useful rule of thumb is this:

If you can clearly define every step of the process up front, or if the outcome is purely informational, an agent is probably not needed.

Responsible AI design is not about using the most capable system available. It's about choosing the system that fits the problem, balancing flexibility, reliability, cost, and impact.

When an App Is the Better Interface

Let me throw a curveball at you. In many cases, the right solution isn't conversational at all.

Applications excel when users need to view, edit, compare, or manage structured information. They provide clarity, control, and predictability, especially when users need to make deliberate choices or review data before taking action.

This is where teams often overreach with agents.

If a user needs to

- Review multiple records side by side

- Enter structured data

- Make explicit selections

- Understand system state at a glance

...an app is usually a better primary interface than conversation.

Conversation is efficient for expressing intent, but it isn't always efficient for decision-making. Asking an agent to walk a user through a complex, multi-step process via chat can introduce friction, ambiguity, and unnecessary back-and-forth.

Here's a quick guide:

If the user would benefit from seeing the information, not just describing it, an app should be part of the solution.

Apps and Agents Work Best Together

This doesn't mean agents and apps are mutually exclusive. In fact, they often work best together.

Apps provide structure. Users can see what's happening, review information, and make deliberate decisions.

Agents, on the other hand, add flexibility. They help interpret intent, guide users, and handle exceptions when the path forward isn't obvious. When combined with an app, an agent becomes a coordinator and assistant, not the sole interface.

In this pattern, the app remains the system of record, while the agent helps users work within it.

An agent embedded in an app might

- Explain what action is needed and why

- Answer questions about data, policies, or context

- Summarize large or complex datasets

- Help map unstructured input into structured fields

- Assist when a user gets stuck or isn't sure how to proceed

The app, meanwhile, provides

- Visibility into records and current state

- Clear display for review, approval, or input

- Confidence that users understand what they are acting on

You can see this pattern emerging in platforms like Power Apps, where agents are increasingly built directly into the app experience. These agents can help users summarize data shown in the app, search across records using natural language, or even paste in unstructured text and have it mapped to the appropriate fields in a data source. The user remains in a familiar, structured interface, while the agent reduces friction and cognitive load.

This combination is especially powerful for onboarding and adoption. Enterprise systems often come with their own terminology, processes, and assumptions. New users may not know what a field means, why a step is required, or how to recover from a mistake. An agent embedded in the app acts like an expert guide, helping users learn the system as they use it, rather than forcing them to go searching through external documentation or training.

The result is a more approachable system without sacrificing control. The app enforces structure and governance. The agent provides assistance, explanation, and flexibility. Together, they create experiences that are both powerful and usable.

Over-conversationalizing Work

One of the most common design mistakes in AI systems is forcing every interaction to go through a conversation.

Not everything needs to be asked, clarified, or confirmed in chat. When systems rely too heavily on conversational interaction, users can lose situational awareness and confidence in the outcome.

We must always remind ourselves of the goal. The goal isn't to make everything conversational. The goal is to make *work easier.*

Sometimes that means conversation. Sometimes that means automation. And sometimes it means a good old-fashioned, well-designed app, with AI working quietly in the background.

Combining Patterns Thoughtfully

In general, the most effective systems combine these patterns.

A chatbot may serve as the entry point. AI automation may help interpret input. An agent may reason about next steps. Workflows may execute actions reliably.

Understanding the strengths and limits of each pattern makes it easier to make better design choices.

With these decision points in mind, let's walk through a concrete scenario to see how each pattern behaves in practice.

One Scenario, Four Approaches

To make the differences between chatbots, workflows, AI automation, and agents more concrete, let's walk through the same real-world scenario handled four different ways.

We'll keep the scenario intentionally simple and intentionally messy. An employee sends the following email:

> "Hey, I'm going to be out the last week of March. Can you make sure everything is taken care of?"

There's no form submission. No subject line that says, "PTO Request." No explicit dates defined.

Now let's see how each approach handles it.

Approach 1: Chatbot

A traditional chatbot interacts through conversation, so, for the sake of this scenario, let's assume the employee also types in that same request into the chatbot. The chatbot may respond with something like

> "To request time off, please submit the time off form."

This response is technically correct, but it misses the point. The chatbot doesn't recognize that a PTO request has already been implied. It doesn't extract dates. It doesn't check policy. It simply routes the user to a known path. So for this scenario, it isn't going to cut it.

Approach 2: Workflow

A workflow excels at execution once it's been triggered.

In this scenario, the workflow might be designed to run when

- A PTO form is submitted

- An email subject contains specific keywords

- A field is populated in a system of record

Because the original email doesn't meet those conditions, the workflow never runs.

From the workflow's perspective, nothing happened.

This isn't a failure of automation; it's a limitation of determinism. The workflow does exactly what it was told to do. It just wasn't told to do anything in this case.

Approach 3: AI Automation (The Bridge)

AI automation introduces intelligence at the point where deterministic systems usually fail.

In this pattern, AI could be used to interpret unstructured input, in this case, the email, while a workflow still handles execution.

The system reads the message and classifies it as a likely PTO request. It extracts a time range ("last week of March") and determines that an approval process should begin. Once that determination is made, a workflow is triggered to record the request and route it for approval.

The automation hasn't changed. The steps are still deterministic and repeatable. What's changed is how the trigger was identified.

This approach is more resilient than chatbots or workflows alone, but it still has limits. If the dates are ambiguous, if policy exceptions apply, or if clarification is needed, the system may still fall short.

AI automation improves when automation runs, but it doesn't yet manage the entire problem.

Approach 4: Agent

An agent handles the scenario differently.

When the email arrives, the agent interprets it as a PTO request, but it doesn't execute anything immediately. Instead, it reasons about what's missing and what matters next.

The agent may respond with a follow-up question:

> "I can help with that. Can you confirm the exact dates you'll be out, and whether this is vacation or another type of leave?"

Once the employee replies, the agent checks company policy, verifies that the request is valid, checks the time tracking system to ensure the employee has enough time off remaining, and then triggers the appropriate workflow to record the time off and route it for approval.

Throughout the process, the agent isn't inventing behavior. It's operating within defined boundaries, using approved knowledge, following rules, and invoking workflows where needed. What's different is that the agent decides *how to move the request forward* rather than relying on a single predefined trigger. This is exactly what we need in this scenario.

So, What Is Copilot, Really?

Now that we have a better understanding of agents, workflows, and chatbots, we can begin to answer the question that started this whole chapter, what exactly is Copilot?

Copilot isn't just a chatbot.

It's not a single agent.

And it's not a workflow tool.

Copilot is a **platform** that brings conversation, reasoning, and execution together. This is why Copilot feels different from previous tools: it doesn't just respond or automate, it connects understanding, reasoning, and execution in a single experience.

Within Copilot

- Chat interfaces capture user requests and signals of intent

- AI interprets unstructured input

- Agents reason and choose actions

- Workflows execute deterministic steps

That's why Copilot can feel conversational one moment and operational the next. It's not one thing; it's an environment where multiple patterns work together.

Summary and Key Takeaways

This chapter unpacked the systems that sit behind conversational experiences and clarified how chatbots, workflows, AI automation, and agents each play distinct roles. While they often appear similar on the surface, they differ in how they interpret intent, make decisions, and execute work. Understanding these differences is essential to understanding what Copilot actually is and what it isn't.

Rather than replacing existing patterns, Copilot brings them together. It uses conversation as an entry point, AI to interpret messy human input, agents to reason about goals and next steps, and workflows to execute actions reliably. Each component builds on the last, expanding what's possible without sacrificing control.

Key takeaways:

- **Chatbots manage conversation, not execution.**
  Traditional chatbots rely on predefined logic, while
  AI-powered chatbots use language models to respond
  more flexibly, but neither is responsible for ensuring
  work gets done correctly end to end.

- **Workflows excel at reliable execution**. They perform
  predefined steps consistently and predictably, but they
  require structured triggers and don't interpret intent on
  their own.

- **AI automation enhances workflows without
  replacing them.** AI can be used before, during, or after
  workflow steps to classify input, summarize content, or
  extract information, while the workflow itself remains
  deterministic.

- **Agents introduce reasoning into the system.** Agents
  don't just respond or trigger automation; they reason
  about goals, ask clarifying questions, and decide how to
  move work forward within defined boundaries.

- **Copilot isn't a single thing**. It's a platform that
  combines conversation, AI reasoning, agents, and
  workflows into a unified experience, which is why it
  can feel conversational one moment and operational
  the next.

With these concepts in place, we go a bit deeper. In the next chapter,
we'll focus specifically on agents: how they are structured, how they're
constrained, and how Copilot Studio enables you to build them without
having to write a bunch of code.

CHAPTER 5

The Agent Builder's Toolbox

For as long as I've worked in tech, there's been a tug-of-war: low code versus pro-code.

On one side, you have developers armed with C#, JavaScript, Python, etc., sometimes skeptical of drag-and-drop tools. On the other hand, business users and domain experts see real problems every day and want to solve them without waiting months for IT backlogs to clear.

In this AI era, the tension hasn't necessarily disappeared, but it has changed. It's no longer low-code *or* pro-code; it's low-code *and* pro-code, often blended through AI-assisted and "vibe-coded" experiences. Nowhere is that more evident than in the world of AI agents.

Microsoft's Copilot ecosystem gives us multiple on-ramps for building agents, depending on your skillset and the problem you're trying to solve. An HR manager shouldn't need to write C# to build a simple HR policy agent. At the same time, an engineering team may need far more control over orchestration, integrations, and state management than a configuration-only, out-of-the-box experience can provide.

This chapter is about understanding **those trade-offs**.

We'll explore

- When you shouldn't build an agent at all

© April Dunnam 2026

A. Dunnam, *The Copilot Compass*, https://doi.org/10.1007/979-8-8688-2655-9_5

- The difference between **declarative agents** and **custom engine agents**

- How **Copilot Studio** acts as the bridge between these

- When to use each approach

- The differences in low code and pro code approaches

This chapter intentionally focuses on agents built within the Microsoft 365 Copilot ecosystem. While it is possible to build fully custom agents in Azure or other platforms, those approaches fall outside the scope of this book. When they are mentioned, it's to establish boundaries and decision points, not to provide implementation guidance.

Build vs. Use: Knowing When Not to Build an Agent

Before we talk about *how* to build an agent, we need to talk about when **not** to build one.

Just because you can build something doesn't mean you should.

In traditional software, this is often framed as the "build versus buy" decision.

With Copilot and agents, a similar question applies:

Should you build a custom agent, or does one already exist that meets your needs?

Microsoft 365 Copilot includes a growing set of out-of-the-box agents designed for common business scenarios. These agents are deeply integrated into Microsoft 365, benefit from Microsoft-managed grounding and security, and are continuously improved by Microsoft.

Examples include agents focused on

- Research and analysis

- Writing and ideation

- People and organizational insights

- Learning and skills

- Administration and app building

- Productivity within Word, Excel, and PowerPoint

There's also an expanding ecosystem of **third-party agents** from vendors such as HR platforms, project management tools, design tools, and content repositories.

Rule of thumb:

If an existing agent already solves 80–90% of your problem, building a custom agent often introduces unnecessary cost, risk, and maintenance.

It's also worth pausing for one more question: do you actually need an *agent* at all?

In the previous chapter, we discussed where agents fit alongside other tools such as chatbots, workflows, and apps. Sometimes what feels like an "agent problem" is really a deterministic automation, a simple chatbot, a well-designed form, or a lightweight app. Agents shine when reasoning, context, and flexibility matter.

Understanding the Types of Agents You Can Build

Once you've decided that a custom agent is justified, the next step is understanding the types of agents you can build.

At a conceptual level, agents often fall into three patterns:

Retrieval-Based Agents

These agents focus on finding and summarizing information from knowledge sources. Their primary role is to ground and synthesize data.

Examples include

- Policy and procedure agents

- Internal documentation assistants

- Knowledge base search agents

Task-Based Agents

Task-based agents go beyond retrieval and can also perform actions.

Examples include

- Creating or updating documents

- Creating images

- Triggering workflows

- Writing data to systems

- Sending emails or notifications

Autonomous Agents

These agents can run without direct user interaction, responding to triggers such as events or schedules.

Examples include

- Monitoring inboxes or document libraries

- Automatically classifying or routing content

- Kicking off agentic workflows based on conditions

Within Microsoft 365 Copilot, these patterns are implemented through **two primary agent categories** (Table 5-1):

Table 5-1. *Agent Categories*

Category	Description
Declarative Agents	Configuration-driven agents where you define intent, knowledge, and allowed tools, and Copilot handles the orchestration
Custom Engine Agents	Agents where you bring your own orchestration logic, tools, or models, while still integrating with Copilot

At this point, it's important to clarify two concepts that are easy to conflate: **agent type** and **build approach**.

Declarative agents and custom engine agents describe *who owns orchestration*. Low-code and pro-code describe *how the agent is authored and hosted*. These are related, but they aren't the same thing.

You can build declarative agents using no-code tools or pro-code approaches. Likewise, you can build custom engine agents using low-code tools like Copilot Studio or fully pro-code solutions. Throughout this chapter, we'll focus on orchestration ownership first and then layer in how low-code and pro-code fit into that picture.

Declarative Agents: The Starting Point

Before we talk about *how* declarative agents work, let's slow down and ask a more fundamental question: **why do declarative agents exist at all?**

The answer has very little to do with convenience and everything to do with orchestration.

If the term *orchestration* feels familiar, it should. In Chapter 3, we introduced orchestration as the layer that decides which models to call, which data to ground responses in, and which tools to use to fulfill a request. Here, we're seeing what that concept looks like in practice, specifically, what happens when orchestration is handled for you by the platform instead of being something every builder must design themselves.

Why Declarative Agents Exist

Short answer: Orchestration is hard.

That might sound obvious, but it's easy to underestimate just how difficult orchestration becomes once AI enters the picture. Traditional software systems follow deterministic paths: if this happens, do that. Workflows, scripts, and traditional chatbots are designed around predictability. Given the same inputs, they produce the same outputs.

AI systems don't work that way.

Large language models are inherently probabilistic. They reason, infer, and generate responses based on patterns rather than fixed rules. That flexibility is what makes them powerful, but it's also what makes them risky when applied directly to business systems.

If every time you wanted to build an agent, you had to decide when to retrieve data, how to sequence actions, which tools to invoke, how to handle failures, and how to respect permissions and compliance boundaries, that would be chaos.

Not just technical chaos, but governance chaos too.

Microsoft's challenge, then, was not simply to make agent building *easier*. It was to make it safer, more scalable, and better suited to the enterprise, especially in environments like Microsoft 365, where agents operate on sensitive data and user-specific context.

Declarative agents are Microsoft's answer to that challenge.

Instead of asking builders to orchestrate every step, declarative agents shift responsibility upward to the platform. Builders describe *what they want the agent to do, what it should know*, and *what it is allowed to use*. Microsoft 365 Copilot takes on the responsibility of deciding *how* to make that happen.

This design choice protects organizations from inconsistent implementations, reduces the likelihood of unsafe behavior, and allows Microsoft to continuously improve orchestration without requiring every agent to be rebuilt.

Declarative agents exist not because orchestration is unimportant but because it's *too important* to leave entirely to individual builders all the time.

What "Declarative" Actually Means

With that context in mind, the idea of a declarative agent becomes a bit clearer.

A declarative agent is one where you define the **intent and boundaries**, not the execution plan.

When building a declarative agent, you focus on defining

- The agent's purpose and instructions

- The knowledge sources it can ground itself in

- The tools it's allowed to use (from a pre-determined selection)

You do **not** define

- The order the steps must run

- How reasoning should be broken down

- How responses should be constructed

That responsibility belongs to Microsoft 365 Copilot.

This is a key distinction, and it's often uncomfortable for experienced developers at first. Giving up control over orchestration can feel like giving up power. In practice, it often results in more reliable, maintainable agents.

Declarative doesn't always mean "simple." It means **you declare the what, not the how**.

What You Gain by Letting Copilot Orchestrate

By leaning on Copilot's orchestration, declarative agents inherit a set of capabilities that would be difficult to reproduce manually:

- **Enterprise-grade security and compliance**, including alignment with Microsoft 365 permissions

- **Permission-aware grounding**, so users only see what they're allowed to see

- **Microsoft-managed orchestration**, which evolves as the platform improves

- **Built-in responsible AI controls**, including safety filters and governance boundaries

These aren't incidental benefits. They're the primary reason declarative agents scale well across organizations.

From an adoption perspective, declarative agents also dramatically lower the barrier to entry. Business users, IT professionals, and builders can build useful agents without needing to understand prompt chaining, state management, or error handling strategies. At the same time, developers retain the option to step in when deeper control is required.

This balance of broad accessibility paired with centralized control is what makes declarative agents such a natural starting point.

Ways to Build Declarative Agents

Declarative agents are defined by **who owns orchestration**, not by how they are authored. Regardless of the tool used, declarative agents all share one defining trait: Microsoft 365 Copilot controls orchestration, while the builder declares intent, grounding, and allowed actions.

There are several approaches for building declarative agents. These options span no-code, low-code, and pro-code, but they all result in the same runtime behavior (Table 5-2).

Table 5-2. *Declarative Agent Approaches*

Tool	Primary audience	Code required	Where the agent runs	When to use
Agent Builder	Business users, builders	No	Microsoft 365 Copilot	Quick wins and simple declarative agents
SharePoint Agents	Business users, builders	No	SharePoint	Document-centric knowledge scenarios
Copilot Studio (Declarative Mode)	Power users, IT, Developers	Low	Microsoft 365 Copilot	Richer configuration without custom orchestration
Microsoft 365 Agents Toolkit	Developers	Yes	Microsoft 365 Copilot	Enterprise-grade declarative agents, CI/CD, advanced integrations

All these tools produce **declarative agents**. The difference lies in *how the agent is authored*, not in its *behavior at runtime*.

Agent Builder

Agent Builder provides the most approachable, no-code entry point for creating declarative agents. It offers a guided experience focused on speed and simplicity.

Agents built with Agent Builder

- Are configured through instructions and knowledge sources

- Rely entirely on Copilot-managed orchestration

- Surface directly inside Microsoft 365 Copilot

This approach is ideal for quick wins, experimentation, and scenarios where builders want to focus exclusively on *what* the agent should do rather than *how* it does it.

SharePoint Agents

SharePoint agents use the same declarative model but are scoped directly to SharePoint sites, pages, or document libraries.

From an authoring perspective, SharePoint agents feel very similar to Agent Builder. The key difference is where the agent lives and how users encounter it. Because these agents are embedded directly into SharePoint, they are especially effective for

- Policies and procedures

- Internal documentation

- Project and team knowledge hubs

They also benefit automatically from SharePoint's permission model, ensuring users only see content they are authorized to access.

Copilot Studio

Copilot Studio offers a more flexible authoring environment while still supporting fully declarative agents.

When used in declarative mode, Copilot Studio allows builders to

- Define more detailed instructions and behaviors

- Connect multiple knowledge sources

- Enable a curated set of actions and tools

- Deploy agents directly into Microsoft 365 Copilot

At this stage, the agent is still declarative. Copilot continues to manage orchestration, reasoning flow, and sequencing. Copilot Studio simply provides a richer configuration surface, making it a natural choice when declarative agents need to grow in sophistication without yet crossing into custom engine territory.

Microsoft 365 Agents Toolkit

The Microsoft 365 Agents Toolkit is the primary pro-code authoring tool for building declarative agents.

It allows developers to

- Define declarative agents using manifests and configuration files

- Build plugins and connectors that expose APIs to Copilot

- Integrate with enterprise systems using code-first practices

- Manage deployments through source control and CI/ CD pipelines

Despite being authored entirely in code, agents built with the Agents Toolkit remain **declarative** as long as

- Copilot retains control over orchestration

- The execution order is not explicitly defined by the developer

- Reasoning and sequencing are handled by the Copilot runtime

This makes the Agents Toolkit the right choice when teams need:

- Repeatable deployments

- Enterprise development practices

- Tight integration with existing services, without taking on full orchestration responsibility

What All Declarative Tools Have in Common

Whether built with no-code tools like Agent Builder, low-code tools like Copilot Studio, or pro-code tools like the Microsoft 365 Agents Toolkit, all declarative agents share the same execution model:

- Builders declare **what the agent should do**

- Copilot decides **how it is done**

- Orchestration remains centralized and platform-managed

This separation is what enables declarative agents to scale safely across organizations, regardless of who builds them or which tools they use.

Why This Is the "Starting Point"

Declarative agents aren't the end all beat all, but they are a natural starting point for many of your agent scenarios. Why? Because they are quick to build and help you validate use cases fast. And they can deliver real value without over-engineering.

As you'll see later in this chapter, there are clear moments when declarative agents begin to show their limits. But starting here is rarely a mistake. In fact, many agent initiatives fail not because declarative agents are insufficient, but because teams skip this step and reach for complexity too early.

Understanding *why* declarative agents exist makes it much easier to recognize when it's time to move beyond them.

When Declarative Agents Start to Crack

Declarative agents provide a powerful and safe way to extend Microsoft 365 Copilot, but they aren't a universal solution. They were designed to let Copilot's built-in orchestrator coordinate the interaction between user instruction, data sources, and available actions.

Once you start needing control over that underlying orchestration, where decisions, sequencing, and workflow behavior must be explicit, you've begun to outgrow the declarative model.

Let's look at some common signals that give you hints that you are outgrowing declarative agents and need to transition to custom engine agents (or other tooling).

Signal 1: You Need Deterministic Workflow Control

Declarative agents let Copilot decide how to interpret intent and sequence reasoning, and actions. But some workflows require *exact, predictable orchestration*, for example:

- Approvals that must occur in a defined order

- Multi-step processes where each step's success determines the next

- Retry or rollback behavior if a step fails

These are not orchestrated by Copilot itself; declarative agents defer orchestration to the platform. When your scenario requires explicit sequencing or conditional execution, Copilot's flexible reasoning is no longer sufficient; you need control over orchestration. Custom engine agents give you that control.

Signal 2: You Are Integrating Multiple Disparate Systems

Declarative agents can be extended with API plugins so they can *interact* with external systems (including REST APIs or MCP servers).
But when your agent must

- Combine data from several systems

- Write data back into one system based on another

- Guarantee ordering and error handling

…you are no longer just adding knowledge to Copilot, you're orchestrating an integration workflow. Copilot's declarative model doesn't give you fine-grained control over that orchestration, but custom engine agents do.

Signal 3: You Want Explicit Tool Invocation Beyond Declarative Actions

Declarative agents allow you to configure knowledge and actions within Copilot's model. They can call out to APIs configured as actions.

But if you need

- Sequence control over those tools

- Conditional logic that determines *when* to invoke which tool

- Structured orchestration of tools as part of a broader workflow

...you're moving beyond Copilot's declarative action model into an orchestration domain that Copilot doesn't expose declaratively. This is another hallmark of scenarios that are better served by a custom engine agent.

Signal 4: Predictability Is Non-Negotiable

Copilot's declarative agents leverage underlying models and reasoning that can change over time as the product evolves. That's a feature for general adaptability, but it becomes a liability when responses and behavior need to be exact and predictable every time.

In regulated industries, compliance workflows, or financial systems where consistent execution matters more than flexible conversation, you need an agent whose behavior you can test and control end to end, another sign it's time to move away from a purely declarative agent.

Signal 5: You Are Repeating Complex Orchestration Logic Outside Copilot

Sometimes teams try to compensate for declarative agent limits by

- Embedding logic in the prompt

- Adding custom actions that attempt to simulate workflow

- Trying to use Copilot's reasoning layer to manage sequencing

These workarounds generally lead to brittle experiences. Declarative agents are not meant for complex orchestration; they are meant for *declarative intent*. When you feel compelled to patch around limitations, it's a signal that you need a different pattern, often a custom engine agent built and orchestrated explicitly in Copilot Studio.

A Practical Rule of Thumb

If your scenario begins to require you to own how things execute, not just what you want, you are crossing the boundary between Copilot-orchestrated behavior and custom orchestration.

In Microsoft's extensibility architecture, that's precisely when you transition from

- **Declarative agents** (Copilot manages orchestration)

  to

- **Custom engine agents** (you manage orchestration, tool sequencing, and workflow logic)

Custom Engine Agents: When You Need to Take Control

Custom engine agents exist for scenarios where letting Copilot decide *how* work gets done isn't cutting it. Instead of relying entirely on Copilot's built-in orchestration layer, you take responsibility for parts, or all, of that orchestration yourself.

This doesn't mean you stop using Copilot. It means you change *what Copilot is responsible for*.

Why Custom Engine Agents Exist

Declarative agents are designed to be safe, scalable, and accessible. To achieve that, Microsoft intentionally limits what builders can control.

That works well until orchestration becomes the problem itself.

Custom engine agents exist because some scenarios demand:

- Deterministic execution

- Explicit sequencing

- State management

- Predictable failure handling

- Tightly controlled integrations

In these cases, flexibility becomes a liability. The platform can't infer your intent safely, and guessing wrong would be worse than doing nothing at all.

Microsoft's extensibility model acknowledges this reality. Rather than forcing every agent into a declarative mold, it provides a way for builders to **bring their own orchestration logic** while still surfacing the agent inside the Copilot experience.

What "Custom Engine" Actually Means

The term *custom engine* can be misleading if you take it too literally.

A custom engine agent does **not** mean

- You trained a new language model

- You replaced Copilot's models

- You built an AI system from scratch

Instead, it means this:

You're no longer relying solely on Copilot to decide how work is executed.

With a custom engine agent, you control

- **When** tools are called

- **In what order** steps run

- **How** data flows between systems

- **What happens** when something fails

Copilot still provides

- The conversational interface

- Access to Microsoft 365 context

- Grounding and identity

- A consistent user experience

But orchestration is no longer opaque. It's intentional.

Practical Examples of Custom Engine Scenarios

Custom engine agents typically show up in scenarios like these:

Deterministic Business Processes

For example, an approval process where

1. A request must be validated

2. A manager must approve

3. A system of record must be updated

4. A confirmation must be sent

Each step must happen in order, and failure at any step must be handled explicitly.

Multi-system Integrations

An agent that

- Reads data from SharePoint

- Updates a CRM

- Triggers a ticketing system

- Logs activity for audit purposes

Here, orchestration is the *core problem*, not conversation.

Explicit Tool Sequencing

An agent that must

- Call a specific API

- Process the result

- Invoke another tool based on structured output

- Call another agent or MCP server

Declarative agents can *access* some tools, but they cannot reliably *coordinate* them.

Regulated or Audited Environments

In finance, healthcare, or compliance-heavy scenarios, teams need

- Repeatable behavior

- Testable logic

- Explainable execution paths

Custom engine agents allow that level of control.

Low-Code vs. Pro-Code Custom Engines

An important clarification: **custom engine does not automatically mean pro-code**.

There are two common ways custom engine agents are built.

Low-Code Custom Engines

Using Copilot Studio, builders can

- Call Power Automate flows

- Invoke APIs via connectors or invoke MCP servers

- Chain tools deterministically

- Manage execution paths visually

In this model, Copilot handles conversation, but execution is explicit and controlled.

Pro-Code Custom Engines

For more advanced scenarios, developers may

- Write orchestration logic in code

- Integrate with systems that have no connectors

- Manage state externally

- Implement advanced monitoring and error handling

Both approaches are valid. The difference is not *who* builds the agent but rather **who owns orchestration**.

What You Trade When You Go Custom

Custom engine agents give you control, but that control comes with responsibility.

When you take ownership of orchestration, you also take ownership of

- Testing and validation

- Error handling and retries

- Monitoring and observability

- Governance and maintenance

This is why custom engine agents are not the starting point. They are a response to complexity, not a default choice.

A Natural Transition Point

By the time teams reach for custom engine agents, they rarely want to abandon declarative agents entirely. Instead, they want a way to

- Keep conversational flexibility

- Retain Copilot's grounding and security

- Selectively take control where needed

This is exactly the role Copilot Studio plays.

In the next section, we'll look at Copilot Studio as the bridge between declarative and custom engine agents, and why it's best thought of not as a single tool but as a progression path from low code to pro-code.

Copilot Studio: The Gateway Between Declarative and Custom Engine Agents

Copilot Studio sits at the **center of agent development** in Microsoft 365.

Copilot Studio isn't a single "agent type." It's an **agent development platform**. One that intentionally spans both low-code and pro-code approaches. You're not choosing between a declarative *or* a custom engine when you open Copilot Studio. You're choosing **how much orchestration you want to own.**

Microsoft could have drawn a hard line:

- Declarative agents for business users

- Custom engine agents for developers

But real-world scenarios don't evolve that cleanly.
Most agent projects start simple:

- Answer questions

- Summarize documents

- Help users find information

Over time, those same agents often need to

- Call deterministic workflows

- Integrate with line-of-business systems

- Handle failures explicitly

- Run in channels outside Microsoft 365

Copilot Studio exists to support that natural progression, without forcing teams to throw away what they've already built.

Copilot Studio and Declarative Agents

At its simplest, Copilot Studio can be used to build purely declarative agents.

In this mode, you define instructions and behavior, connect knowledge sources, and Copilot owns the orchestration.

Behind the scenes, these agents still rely entirely on Microsoft 365 Copilot's built-in orchestration layer. Copilot decides which model to use, when to retrieve grounding data, and how to compose responses.

In other words, Copilot Studio doesn't automatically make an agent "custom." It can simply be a more flexible authoring surface for declarative agents that are ultimately deployed into Microsoft 365 Copilot.

Where Copilot Studio Becomes a Custom Engine Environment

Copilot Studio becomes a custom engine environment the moment you start taking back orchestration responsibility.

This happens when you introduce elements such as

- Power Automate flows for deterministic execution

- Explicit sequencing of tools

- Conditional branching based on structured outputs

- Integration with external systems or MCP servers

At that point, Copilot is no longer deciding *how* work is executed. It's participating in a workflow that **you control.**

Copilot still handles the chat interaction, maintains conversational context, and surfaces results to the user.

But orchestration is now intentional, explicit, and owned by the builder. That is the defining characteristic of a custom engine agent, regardless of whether it's built with low-code or pro-code.

Pro-Code Extensibility

For more advanced scenarios, Copilot Studio doesn't block pro developers; it enables them.

Developers can call API's or MCP servers that have no prebuilt connectors and even incorporate specialized models hosted in Azure.

These models and services can be invoked as part of the agent's execution flow, while Copilot Studio continues to act as the integration point and conversational front end.

This aligns with Microsoft's extensibility approach: Copilot remains the experience layer, while execution logic can live wherever it makes the most sense.

Deployment Inside Microsoft 365 and Beyond

Another key reason Copilot Studio is central to the agent ecosystem is where agents can be deployed.

Agents built with Copilot Studio can be deployed directly in Microsoft 365 Copilot, Microsoft teams, embedded in public or internal websites or to multiple supported messaging channels.

This is an important distinction.

Declarative agents created through Agent Builder or SharePoint are tightly scoped to Microsoft 365. Copilot Studio expands that reach. It allows you to build once and surface the agent wherever users already work, inside or outside Microsoft 365, while still reusing the same orchestration and logic.

Bringing It All Together

Copilot Studio is best understood not as a single tool but as a **spectrum of capabilities**.

- At one end, it supports declarative agents fully orchestrated by Copilot.

- In the middle, it enables shared orchestration through flows and tools.

- At the other end, it supports fully custom engine agents, where execution logic is owned by the builder.

What doesn't change across that spectrum is the user experience. Agents still feel like Copilot. They still respect identity, permissions, and context. The difference is who decides *how* work gets done.

That's why Copilot Studio is the true bridge between low-code and pro-code, and why it plays such a central role in any serious agent strategy.

When Pro-Code Becomes Necessary

Pro-code isn't about prestige; it's about necessity.

Many agent scenarios never need full code. Declarative agents and low-code custom engine agents built in Copilot Studio cover a surprising amount of ground. But there is a clear line where low-code approaches stop being sufficient, not because they're limited, but because the problem itself demands deeper control.

This is the point where pro-code becomes necessary.

What "Pro-Code" Actually Means in This Context

In the context of Microsoft 365 Copilot extensibility, pro-code doesn't mean abandoning Copilot or rebuilding everything from scratch.

It means

- You're building or owning **the execution layer**

- You're responsible for orchestration logic

- You're integrating Copilot with systems, models, or services that can't be expressed declaratively or visually

Pro-code agents still surface inside Copilot. They still participate in the Copilot experience. What changes is where the logic lives and who owns it.

Why Low-Code Sometimes Hits a Ceiling

Copilot Studio's low-code capabilities are powerful but also intentionally bounded. They're designed to help simplify common integrations, express orchestration visually, and reduce the burden of custom development. But sometimes there are requirements that can't be met without some code.

You typically need to step into pro-code when

- Orchestration logic becomes highly stateful

- Execution must be precisely controlled

- Integrations don't map cleanly to connectors or flows

- Performance, scale, or latency becomes critical

- Advanced monitoring, logging, or observability is required

At this point, you're no longer just "configuring an agent." You're building an AI-powered system that happens to use Copilot as its interface.

Pro-Code Building Blocks in the Copilot Extensibility Model

Microsoft's extensibility architecture provides several pro-code entry points, each serving a different purpose.

Agent SDKs

Agent SDKs allow developers to build agents where orchestration logic is written explicitly in code.

Using an SDK, you can

- Control execution flow step by step

- Manage state across interactions

- Decide exactly when and how tools are invoked

- Integrate with custom services and data stores

- Implement advanced error handling and retries

One of the most significant differences when using the SDK is how state is handled. With SDK-based agents, state can be persisted across interactions and over time. This makes it possible to support long-running or multi-phase processes, scenarios where work unfolds across multiple steps, sessions, or systems. Rather than treating each interaction as isolated, the agent can resume, continue, or recover based on previously stored context.

Agent SDKs also enable deeper integrations. Developers can connect directly to custom services, proprietary data stores, or domain-specific systems that don't fit cleanly into standard connectors. Because orchestration logic lives in code, these integrations can be tailored precisely to the needs of the needs rather than adapted to a predefined abstraction.

Another important shift is how reliability is handled. When orchestration is explicitly written, developers can implement advanced error handling, retries, and fallback behavior. This makes agent behavior more predictable and easier to reason about, especially in environments where failures must be handled consistently and transparently.

Agents built with the SDK are appropriate when workflows are complex, span multiple systems, or must follow strict rules. In these cases, business logic needs to be versioned, tested, and audited in the same way as any other production system.

The key distinction is ownership. With SDK-based agents, Copilot no longer owns the engine. It provides the interaction layer and user context, but the developer is responsible for orchestration, execution, and state management.

Copilot Connectors and Plugins

Copilot connectors and plugins are pro-code extensibility points used to expose external systems to Copilot in a structured, secure way.

They allow you to

- Surface proprietary data sources inside Copilot

- Expose APIs as callable actions

- Integrate systems that aren't supported by existing connectors

- Control authentication and authorization explicitly

Compared to low-code connectors, pro-code connectors give you

- More control over request/response shape

- Tighter integration with system-specific logic

- The ability to evolve the integration independently

Connectors don't automatically make an agent "custom engine," but they are often part of a broader pro-code strategy when orchestration and execution live outside Copilot.

Custom Services and External Orchestration

In the most advanced scenarios, Copilot is no longer the system responsible for deciding *how* work is executed. Instead, it becomes one participant in a broader architecture.

In these designs, teams introduce custom services that own orchestration and execution logic. Those services may be written in code, hosted externally, and integrated with enterprise systems or specialized pipelines. Copilot's role shifts from orchestrator to interaction layer, capturing user intent, providing conversational context, and presenting results.

This pattern is common when organizations need to coordinate complex workflows, integrate deeply with existing platforms, or reuse orchestration logic across multiple experiences. For example, a custom service might manage a multi-step business process, invoke specialized models, or enforce domain-specific rules, while Copilot remains the interface through which users interact with that system.

In this architecture, Copilot handles conversation and intent capture, while the external service owns reasoning, execution, state management, and error handling. Results are then returned to Copilot so they can be grounded, contextualized, and presented to the user in a consistent way.

This approach offers the greatest flexibility and architectural control, but it also requires the highest level of ownership. Teams adopting it are effectively building and operating an AI-powered system, with Copilot serving as the front door rather than the engine.

What Changes When You Move to Pro-Code

Stepping into pro-code unlocks capabilities that are difficult or impossible to express visually:

- **Explicit orchestration control**

  You decide exactly what runs, when, and why.

- **Stateful execution**

  You manage memory, persistence, and long-running workflows.

- **Advanced integrations**

  You connect to systems without prebuilt connectors.

- **Custom model usage**

  You invoke specialized or fine-tuned models as part of execution.

- **Observability and governance**

  You log, monitor, test, and audit behavior as you would with any other application.

These benefits come with a cost. Pro-code agents take longer to build, require stronger engineering discipline, and must be actively maintained.

Pro-Code As a Strategic Choice, Not a Default

The biggest mistake teams make is assuming pro-code is the *next step* after low code.

It isn't.

It's a **different lane.**

Low-code and pro-code agents often coexist:

- Declarative agents handle knowledge and discovery

- Low-code custom engines handle common workflows

- Pro-code agents handle mission-critical custom execution needs

The most mature Copilot implementations intentionally mix all three.

Decision Framework: Choosing the Right Tool

By now, we've explored declarative agents, custom engine agents, Copilot Studio, and when pro-code becomes necessary. The remaining challenge is a practical one: **how do you decide which approach to use for a real business scenario?**

Rather than thinking in terms of tools, it's more useful to think in terms of *requirements*. The scenarios below illustrate common patterns and show how different agent approaches naturally fit different needs.

Scenario 1: HR Policy and Benefits Questions

The situation

An HR team wants to help employees understand policies related to benefits, time off, and internal procedures. The information already lives in SharePoint and changes occasionally, but the questions are largely informational.

The temptation

Build a complex agent that can reason deeply, track history, and escalate issues.

The reality

This is primarily a knowledge retrieval and interpretation problem.

Best fit

- Declarative agent

- Built using Agent Builder or SharePoint Agents

Why this works

- Declarative agents excel at grounding responses in documents

- SharePoint permissions automatically control access

- No explicit orchestration is required

- The agent can reason over multiple documents without custom logic

This is a classic example where starting with declarative avoids unnecessary complexity while still delivering real value.

Scenario 2: Sales Proposal Assistant

The situation

A sales organization wants an assistant that helps account executives

- Answer questions about pricing guidelines

- Summarize recent proposals and statements of work

- Trigger a standard follow-up email or proposal template after a meeting

Most of the content lives in SharePoint and OneDrive. The follow-up steps are consistent and not overly complex.

The temptation

Build a fully custom agent because "it needs actions."

The reality

This is still primarily a conversational and contextual scenario, with a small amount of deterministic execution.

Best fit

- **Declarative agent**, extended with **Copilot Studio**

- Light use of **Power Automate flows** for standard actions

Why this works

- Declarative grounding handles proposal and pricing content well

- Copilot Studio allows deterministic actions like sending emails

- Copilot still owns the conversational flow

- The solution stays accessible to sales ops and power users

This is a classic example of declarative first, with selective orchestration added where needed. A fully custom engine agent would add orchestration overhead without improving outcomes, while a purely declarative agent would struggle to guarantee follow-up actions.

Scenario 3: Employee Onboarding Task Coordinator

The situation

An HR operations team wants an onboarding assistant that

- Creates a new employee record

- Provisions accounts

- Assigns mandatory training

- Notifies managers when steps are complete

Each step depends on the previous one succeeding.

The temptation

Keep expanding a declarative agent with more instructions and actions.

The reality

The core problem here isn't answering questions; it's coordinating a multi-step process across systems.

Best fit

- Custom engine agent

- Built using Copilot Studio with flows and connectors

Why this works

- Execution order matters

- Failures must be handled explicitly

- State needs to be tracked across steps

- Copilot still provides a conversational interface for HR and managers

This is a clear point where declarative agents start to crack, and you need explicit orchestration.

Scenario 4: Finance Approval Agent

The situation

A finance team needs an agent to help with capital expenditure requests. The agent must

- Validate submitted information against internal systems

- Route approvals in a defined order

- Log decisions for audit purposes

- Ensure the same process is followed every time

The temptation

Leverage Copilot's reasoning to "figure it out."

The reality

Flexibility is a liability in regulated workflows. Predictability is mandatory.

Best fit

- Custom engine agent

- Likely involving pro-code orchestration

Why this works

- Deterministic execution is non-negotiable

- Every step must be traceable and testable

- Error handling must be explicit

- Copilot acts as the interface, not the decision-maker

This is where pro-code becomes a requirement, not a preference.

A Better Way to Decide: Ownership, Not Tools

Rather than starting with tools, the most reliable way to choose an agent approach is to start with **ownership**. Specifically: *who should be responsible for decisions, execution, and failure handling?*

The questions below are designed to surface that responsibility.

1. **Who Should Own Orchestration?**

   Ask yourself whether it's acceptable for Copilot to decide *how* work gets done.

   If you're comfortable letting the platform

- Determine execution order

- Choose when tools are invoked

- Adapt behavior as models evolve

Then a **declarative agent**, regardless of how it's built, is usually the right starting point.

If your scenario requires you to explicitly define sequencing, branching, retries, or rollback behavior, you are moving into **custom engine territory**, even if you express that logic using low-code tools.

2. **How Predictable Does the Outcome Need to Be?**

Some scenarios benefit from flexibility. Others demand consistency.

If it's acceptable for responses to vary slightly based on context and reasoning, declarative agents work well. If the outcome must be the same every time, especially in regulated, audited, or transactional workflows, you'll need to take ownership of execution logic.

This is often the point where teams move from declarative agents to custom engine agents, and sometimes further into pro-code implementations.

3. **Where Does the Intelligence Live?**

Consider where the "smarts" of the solution actually belong.

If the intelligence primarily comes from

- Documents

- Microsoft 365 context

- Copilot's reasoning capabilities

Then keeping orchestration with Copilot makes sense.

If intelligence lives in

- External systems

- Specialized models

- Domain-specific services

Copilot often works best as the interaction layer, with orchestration and execution handled elsewhere.

4. **How Much Responsibility Are You Willing to Take On?**

   Every step away from declarative agents increases responsibility. This isn't inherently a bad thing, but if you don't need an elevated level of control, declarative approaches will be easier.

Summary and Key Takeaways

In this chapter, we explored the agent builder's toolbox through the lens of orchestration, responsibility, and trade-offs. Rather than treating low-code and pro-code as opposing camps, Microsoft's Copilot ecosystem allows them to work together, each playing a role at different stages of complexity.

The most effective agent strategies don't start with technology choices. They start with understanding the problem, the level of control required, and who should own execution. Declarative agents provide a safe and scalable entry point. Custom engine agents offer control when orchestration matters. Copilot Studio connects those worlds, enabling teams to grow without starting over.

Key Takeaways

- Declarative agents exist to make AI agent building safer, scalable, and enterprise-ready by centralizing orchestration.

- When you need explicit control over sequencing, state, or failure handling, declarative agents will start to crack.

- Custom engine agents don't replace Copilot; they shift orchestration responsibility to the builder.

- Copilot Studio is the gateway that supports both declarative and custom engine agents and enables gradual progression.

- Pro-code becomes necessary when execution must be deterministic, testable, or deeply integrated with external systems.

- Mature solutions often combine declarative, low-code, and pro-code approaches within a single Copilot experience.

With these patterns in mind, you're now equipped to choose the right tool for the right scenario, and to build agents that scale.

CHAPTER 6

Use Cases, Pitfalls, and the Road Ahead

We've spent this book exploring what Copilot is, how it works, and how far it can be extended. We've gone under the hood, examined orchestration, models, and unpacked what's possible when Copilot connects to your data, workflows, and systems.

But none of that matters if Copilot doesn't actually help you.

If you can't point to a handful of scenarios where Copilot actually saves time, reduces friction, or improves your work life, it risks becoming just another shiny tool. Something people try once, talk about enthusiastically for a couple of weeks, and quietly abandon.

I've noticed that reactions to Copilot tend to cluster at two extremes. On one end are champions who use it constantly and swear by it. On the other end are skeptics who tried it briefly, didn't see immediate value, or decided the cost or risk wasn't worth it. Most people live in the messy middle: they've found a few helpful moments but not the transformational experience they keep hearing about.

This chapter is about closing that gap.

Not by introducing more features.

Not by diagramming more architectures.

But by grounding the conversation in what's actually happening inside real organizations.

A. Dunnam, *The Copilot Compass*, https://doi.org/10.1007/979-8-8688-2655-9_6

I've spoken with practitioners across energy, cybersecurity, and insurance who are actively rolling out Copilot in large, complex enterprises. Their titles and tech stacks differ, but their experiences rhyme in surprising ways.

This chapter distills those field lessons: the patterns that show up when Copilot succeeds, the conditions that cause it to stall, where agents truly earn their keep, and where the hype outpaces reality.

The goal isn't to convince you to use Copilot everywhere.

It's to help you use it well.

What Actually Works: Lessons from Copilot in the Wild

Someone pastes a wall of text into Copilot and types

"Summarize this."

They get a generic response.

They shrug.

Copilot is overrated.

That small moment plays out inside organizations every day. And it quietly determines whether Copilot becomes a daily productivity amplifier or a forgotten experiment.

These are the patterns that showed up repeatedly in real organizations. They show what actually worked. What consistently slowed things down. And what changed as people moved from curiosity to competence.

If there's a single takeaway from my interviews with real-world Copilot users, it's this:

Copilot success has far less to do with clever prompts or flashy demos than it does with expectations, data, and organizational habits.

Let's start with the biggest trap.

Pattern #1: The Expectation Trap

Most early Copilot failures aren't failures of the tooling. They're expectation failures.

A digital transformation leader at a Fortune 500 energy company described what she saw early on: people would paste large amounts of content into Copilot and simply say, "summarize this." When the output wasn't immediately useful, they concluded Copilot wasn't very good.

Nothing was technically broken. What was missing was intent.

People hadn't learned how to articulate what they actually needed:

Summarize for whom?

For what purpose?

At what level of detail?

Once users became more specific about their goals, the quality of results improved dramatically.

A solutions architect at a major insurance company observed a related anti-pattern: people tried Copilot once, got mediocre results, and mentally locked in that verdict forever. But Copilot isn't static. Models change. Capabilities improve. Something that failed last quarter may work well today.

On the opposite extreme, he also saw people expecting Copilot to do everything, from numerical forecasting to deterministic calculations to complex decisioning without recognizing that different tools exist for different kinds of problems. Machine learning models, rules engines, workflows, and LLMs all have strengths. Copilot is not a universal hammer.

He also described the risk of "one-and-done evaluation." Early on, he was frustrated with the quality of image generation and nearly wrote Copilot off entirely. But capabilities improved quickly. The lesson wasn't "images are hard." It was that Copilot is a moving target. If you treat one failure as a permanent verdict, you'll miss the moments where it becomes a genuine productivity saver.

Across all these examples, the pattern is consistent. When Copilot disappoints early, it's usually because

- Users don't yet know how to express intent

- Expectations don't match the tool's strengths

- Integrations are blocked or aren't actually functioning

What this means for you

- Treat early disappointment as a signal to adjust expectations, not abandon the tool.

- Teach that Copilot is iterative, not one-and-done.

- When something fails, ask: *Is this a prompt issue, a capability mismatch, an integration issue, or a technology issue?*

Getting past the expectation trap unlocks the next shift.

Pattern #2: The Outcome Shift

Early-stage Copilot usage often sounds like this:

"Write this email."

"Summarize this document."

"Create a slide deck."

Mature Copilot usage sounds different:

"Help me explain this decision to leadership."

"Surface risks I might be missing."

"Compare these two approaches and show trade-offs."

That shift, from tasks to outcomes, showed up in every interview.

At the energy company, users gradually moved from asking Copilot to perform actions to articulating the result they were trying to achieve. As soon as that happened, Copilot became far more useful.

At the insurance company, the solutions architect described realizing that Copilot works best as a conversation. You don't need a perfect mega-prompt. You start, see what you get, refine, ask follow-up questions, and sometimes even start a fresh chat once you understand the problem better.

At the cybersecurity company, most users initially treated Copilot as search. Over time, they expanded into content generation, and eventually into creating agents for repeatable workflows.

This progression marks the moment Copilot stops being treated like a vending machine and becomes a thinking partner.

One leader summarized it simply:

>AI doesn't replace thinking.

>It amplifies it.

What this means for you

- Teach users to describe outcomes, not just actions.

- Encourage conversational prompting.

- Normalize iteration as success, not failure.

Once people get over the expectation trap and start focusing on outcomes, a new bottleneck appears.

Pattern #3: Data Hygiene Is the Silent Killer

Copilot can't distinguish signal from noise if your organization can't.

At the energy company, a major barrier was the lack of shared best practices combined with large amounts of ROT (redundant, obsolete, and trivial data). Copilot had access to mountains of content but lacked an inherent way to know which documents represented the current truth.

Teams were effectively being forced to define real procedures and standards for the first time.

At the insurance company, the organization invested heavily in SharePoint-based knowledge bases and standard operating procedures. Copilot and SharePoint agents could then answer questions directly from those sources, often with citations.

The difference between "Copilot is useless" and "Copilot is amazing" wasn't the model.

It was the quality and organization of the knowledge behind it.

At the cybersecurity company, tool sprawl created a similar challenge. Teams used Notion, Glean, and Copilot for overlapping purposes. Users assumed Copilot lacked features that other tools had, when in reality, integrations and configuration were the limiting factor.

You simply can't prompt your way out of messy information. As the old saying goes, "garbage in, garbage out."

What this means for you

- Identify a small set of trusted knowledge sources to start.

- Invest in cleaning and curating those sources.

- Treat knowledge management as part of your ongoing AI strategy.

Good data doesn't guarantee success.

Bad data almost always guarantees failure.

Pattern #4: Security and Integration Decide the Ceiling

It's easy to frame Copilot adoption as a user problem.

People need better prompts.

People need training.

People need to try harder.

In practice, many "user problems" are really infrastructure problems.

A product director at an enterprise cybersecurity and IT operations company learned this quickly when he tried querying Salesforce through Copilot. He assumed calling the Salesforce connector would be straightforward. Instead, the experiment failed.

Why? IT and security had blocked the integration.

From the user's perspective, Copilot was broken.

In reality, Copilot never had permission to do the work.

When integrations are blocked, misconfigured, or partially deployed, users don't experience "limited access." They experience "Copilot doesn't work." Over time, that perception hardens into belief.

A solutions architect in insurance described a more staged approach. Their organization began by allowing employees to use Copilot chat, which was already covered by existing identity and data protection policies. Only later did they expand into Microsoft 365 Copilot licenses, starting with some select power users who were eager to experiment with what it could do.

That sequencing turned out to be a key to success. People encountered Copilot in safe, supported ways before being asked to trust it with deeper access to enterprise systems.

A digital transformation leader in energy saw a similar pattern: adoption accelerated most when people were simply given access and allowed to experiment safely. Heavy-handed gatekeeping slowed momentum. Total absence of guardrails created risk. The balance point was clear policies plus low-friction access.

Across organizations, the lesson repeats:

> Copilot's perceived intelligence is capped by what
> it's allowed to touch.

What this means for you

- Treat integrations as first-class adoption work, not a backend detail.

- Make it obvious which systems Copilot can access and which it cannot.

- When something fails, investigate plumbing before blaming prompts.

You can't out-prompt a blocked connector.

Pattern #5: Communities Beat Training

Most organizations start a Copilot rollout with training.

Slide decks.

Recorded sessions.

Documentation.

And sure, those definitely help, but they aren't what creates momentum.

A digital transformation leader in energy described running lunch-and-learns, prompt-sharing sessions, and learning circles. Useful, but not transformative on their own. What made the real difference was giving people access and creating a psychologically safe space to experiment.

Once people tried Copilot with real work, adoption took care of itself.

A product director in cybersecurity echoed this. Their AI team hosts lunch-and-learns and Copilot office hours. People come with real problems, not theoretical questions. The conversation is grounded in "what I tried," "what broke," and "what worked."

A solutions architect in insurance went further, describing the creation of internal Copilot cohorts, essentially user groups. The structure was intentionally lightweight:

- One short presentation or demo

- Plenty of time for open discussion

- Regular cadence (often monthly)

In large enterprises, some cohorts are organized by department. In smaller companies, a single cross-functional group may make more sense.

The magic isn't in the format. It's in normalization.

When people hear peers talk openly about failures, half-working prompts, and incremental wins, experimentation becomes acceptable. Curiosity becomes contagious.

Some organizations layer in additional reinforcement:

- Prompt-of-the-week spotlights

- Internal prompt libraries

- Repositories of reusable instructions or agents

- Occasional contests or recognition

None of this requires perfection, and iteration is expected.

What this means for you

- Create at least one recurring forum for Copilot discussion.

- Prioritize conversation over presentation.

- Encourage sharing imperfect examples.

- Expect things to evolve.

Copilot spreads as a practice, not as a product.

Pattern #6: What Gets Measured Gets Funded

There's a moment most organizations hit somewhere along their Copilot rollout. The early enthusiasm has settled. A handful of people are genuinely getting value from it. But when leadership asks whether the investment is working, no one has a clear answer.

That gap between real but diffuse value and demonstrable business impact is where many Copilot initiatives quietly lose momentum.

In late 2025, reports emerged that Microsoft had cut internal sales targets for its Copilot and agentic AI software by as much as 50% in some cases, after struggling to find enterprise buyers willing to sustain the investment. The problem wasn't simply that the tools were underperforming. It was that organizations couldn't clearly articulate what they were getting for their money. When you can't demonstrate value, it's difficult to justify continued spend and difficult to sustain the behavioral change that adoption requires.

This is a pattern that shows up within organizations long before it appears in sales forecasts.

The challenge here is mostly structural. Traditional ROI frameworks weren't built for tools like Copilot. Time savings with Copilot are real but are often self-reported. Quality improvements are meaningful but subjective. The counterfactual how long would this have taken without Copilot, is difficult to measure cleanly.

What I've seen work is shifting from trying to prove ROI to building a consistent picture of adoption and impact over time.

The solutions architect at the insurance company described a gradual shift in his team's thinking about Copilot's value. Early on, the focus was on individual experimentation, identifying power users, tracking who had licenses, and watching which cohorts were most active. Over time, that evolved into something more systematic: understanding which use cases were generating genuine efficiency, and which ones were creating more work than they saved. The clarity didn't come from a single measurement. It came from paying attention over time and being honest about what was and wasn't working.

That kind of structured visibility is now built directly into Microsoft's tooling. The **Copilot Control System**, part of the Microsoft 365 admin center, provides organizations with a dedicated measurement and reporting layer for Copilot and agents. Through these analytics, IT leaders and business stakeholders can track adoption trends, monitor user engagement with Copilot, and measure behavioral shifts.

For organizations managing agents at scale, **Microsoft Agent 365** extends that visibility further. It provides a central control pane for registering agents, managing access and security, monitoring usage and spend in real time, and setting budget thresholds. Rather than guessing whether an agent is being used and what it's costing, organizations can see exactly how agents are performing and adjust accordingly.

The tooling matters, but it only helps if you know what you're trying to show.

The most effective approach isn't to measure everything; it's to identify a small number of specific use cases where Copilot is deliberately used and to track the impact of those cases in business terms. Not hours saved in the abstract, but drafts reviewed before a key customer proposal. Not prompts submitted, but reports produced without a three-day delay. The digital transformation leader at the energy company described how Copilot's value became undeniable during performance review cycles where the combination of recall, synthesis, and contextual drafting helped leaders connect actions to outcomes in ways that were visible and credible to stakeholders who weren't close to the day-to-day work.

That's the translation that matters most: from personal productivity to organizational evidence.

Adoption that can be articulated survives budget reviews. Adoption that lives only in individual experience tends not to.

What this means for you

- Don't wait for a perfect ROI framework, start tracking adoption behaviors and specific use cases from the beginning.

- Use the Copilot Control System to make adoption visible to IT and business stakeholders.

- Identify two or three high-value scenarios and measure those specifically, in business terms, not just usage counts.

- Translate individual wins into organizational evidence and find the moments where Copilot's impact is visible to people who weren't in the room.

Where Agents Earn Their Keep

By the time organizations reach the point where they have clear expectations, outcome-focused prompting, decent data hygiene, and working integrations, another question starts to surface:

Where do agents meaningfully help?

Not in theory.

Not in demos.

In real work.

A product director in cybersecurity described building a custom agent within Copilot to support market analysis. The prompt itself was nearly two pages long. It encoded a thinking process: what sources to look at, what dimensions to analyze, and how to structure findings.

Before, market analysis was a three-week-long, manually intensive research process. The agent cut that time in half and provided a tool to achieve consistent, repeatable results.

At an insurance company, most agent work centers on GitHub Copilot. They've created agents for code generation, code reviews, security analysis, and documentation. On the Microsoft 365 side, teams started with SharePoint-based knowledge agents and are now exploring customization through Copilot Studio.

The pattern is consistent:

> Agents succeed when they capture repeatable cognition.
>
> Not vague goals.
>
> Not "do everything" mandates.
>
> Specific, scoped, valuable processes.

A useful way to think about it is as a ladder:

Retrieval agents

Answer questions grounded in trusted sources.

Task agents

Perform discrete actions across systems.

Autonomous agents

Chain steps together toward a goal with oversight.

Most organizations start (and should start) at the bottom.

Trying to jump straight to autonomy without strong retrieval and task foundations usually ends in disappointment.

What this means for you

- Identify high-value processes you repeat frequently.

- Start with retrieval or task agents.

- Add autonomy only where guardrails exist.

- Treat agents as stored expertise, not digital employees.

The Copilot Adoption Maturity Curve

After multiple interviews with organizations at different stages of AI adoption, another consistent pattern became clear:

Successful Copilot adoption doesn't happen all at once.

Teams don't flip a switch and suddenly operate with fleets of intelligent agents orchestrating work. Instead, they move through recognizable stages. Each stage delivers real value, and just as importantly, exposes new limitations that naturally push organizations forward.

Here's what that progression typically looks like in practice.

Stage 1: Curiosity and Search

Adoption begins with lightweight experimentation. At this stage, Copilot is often treated as a *fancy search engine*, a faster way to find information, get explanations, or summarize content.

Typical prompts at this stage include

"Summarize this document."

"Explain this concept."

"What does this error mean?"

"What is the timeline for this project?"

Copilot is primarily used to find and digest information more efficiently in Stage 1. This isn't a bad thing. It still provides meaningful value by speeding up understanding, reducing context switching, and helping people feel more confident navigating information.

IIowevcr, there's an inherent risk in staying here too long.

If adoption stalls at this stage, the value can start to feel **incremental rather than transformational**. For some organizations, this is where Copilot is dismissed as "nice to have" rather than worth the investment.

Stage 2: Drafting and Content Acceleration

As comfort grows, people move beyond search into creation.

Once users realize Copilot can not only retrieve information but also understand organizational context, they begin exploring whether it can help them *produce* work, not just consume it.

This is where Copilot starts showing up in

- Email drafting

- Document outlines

- Reports and summaries

- Presentations and meeting follow-ups

At this stage, Copilot begins to feel less like an AI-powered search tool and more like an **editor and co-writer**.

This is often the first moment organizations see noticeable time savings. That blank-page anxiety we all get fades. Writing quality improves. Documentation that once felt tedious becomes easier to produce and easier to maintain.

Limitations at this stage:

- Work is still largely manual.

- Successful prompts are rarely reused.

- Value depends heavily on individual users rather than shared practices.

Stage 3: Socialization and Standardization

Once teams start seeing consistent value from knowledge retrieval and content creation, usage spreads organically.

This is where word of mouth kicks in.

You notice a colleague suddenly producing better-looking PowerPoint decks. Someone else seems to be constantly caught up on emails and meetings. Another teammate is creating custom visuals or summaries at a pace that feels impossible. Eventually, curiosity takes over, and the secret gets shared: *they're using Copilot.*

This is a critical inflection point.

Organizations that succeed here actively nurture internal communities. They encourage people to share what's working, capture successful prompts, and openly discuss what *didn't* work. Shared prompt libraries, informal lunch-and-learns, and internal showcases all help turn individual success into collective momentum.

At this stage, teams also begin exploring **repeatability**. Some experiment with reusable prompt templates, while others dip into simple declarative agents using Agent Builder.

Instead of every user reinventing the wheel, good patterns start to spread.

This stage is still largely user-driven and manually invoked, but it marks a shift from individual experimentation to shared learning and consistency.

Stage 4: Agent Experimentation and Guardrails

At this stage, organizations begin exploring agents more seriously but not yet confidently.

Copilot usage for knowledge retrieval and content creation has become common. Teams have experimented with out-of-the-box agents for tasks like research or analysis, and the idea of custom agents is no longer theoretical. What changes here is **scale**.

More people are building. More agents are appearing. More use cases are being tested.

And with that experimentation comes friction.

Teams begin asking harder questions:

- Should this really be an agent, or would a workflow be better?

- Where does human review need to stay in the loop?

- What data should an agent be allowed to access?

- Who owns this agent once it's deployed?

This stage is defined by **trial and error**.

Some agents prove genuinely valuable. Others feel brittle, over-scoped, or unnecessary. Organizations start to see that not every problem benefits from agentic behavior, and that choosing the right tool matters as much as building the solution itself.

Governance concerns also start to surface here.

As agents integrate with more data sources and systems, questions around access control, testing, monitoring, and accountability become unavoidable. Early enthusiasm gives way to the realization that agents are not just technical artifacts but operational ones.

This is where organizations begin to put guardrails in place, not to slow innovation but to make it sustainable.

Stage 4 is not about perfection. It's about learning where agents help, where they hurt, and where they simply don't belong.

To be successful at this stage is not about building the most agents. It's about learning from what you build.

Stage 5: Operationalized Agents

In the most mature environments, agent usage moves beyond experimentation to operationalization.

Organizations have moved past debating *whether* agents should exist and are now focusing on **how they fit into broader systems**.

Agents are combined with deterministic workflows and external integrations to support end-to-end processes. Clear patterns exist for when to use workflows, when to use agents, and when to blend both.

Organizations at this stage may explore

- Blending agents with workflows for complex processes that need deterministic logic mixed in

- Custom and external integrations through MCP servers

- Carefully scoped autonomous or multi-agent scenarios

The defining characteristic of this stage isn't autonomy; it is **intentional orchestration**.

Governance is operationalized rather than reactive. Organizations have

- Clear ownership

- Defined access models

- Testing and validation processes

- Monitoring and auditing

Humans remain firmly in the loop, focusing on oversight, exception handling, and judgment.

This stage represents stable, scalable adoption.

Not because everything is automated, but because the organization understands **where automation helps and where human intelligence must remain central** (Figure 6-1).

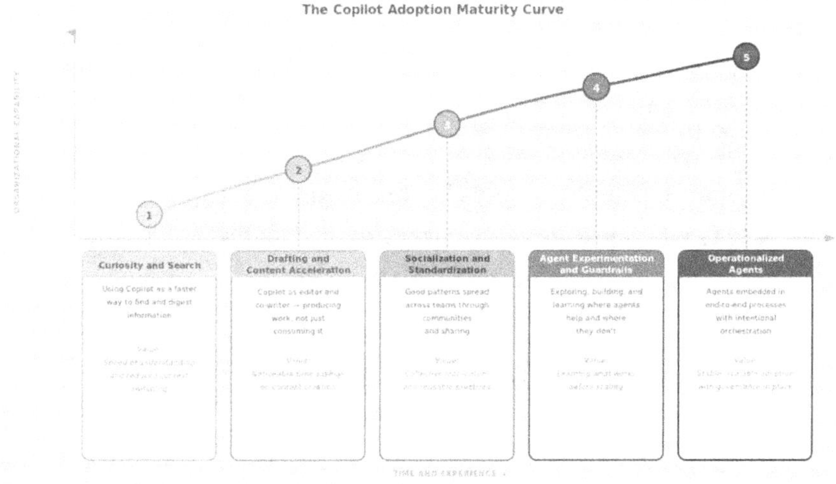

Figure 6-1. *The Copilot Adoption Maturity Curve*

What This Curve Teaches Us

1. Every stage delivers value.

2. No stage should be skipped.

3. Many organizations will live in multiple stages at once.

Progress is not about racing to Stage 5. It's about steadily moving forward while building foundations.

The organizations that I see succeed with Copilot aren't the ones with the most advanced technology. They are the ones that keep climbing.

The Road Ahead

One of the biggest mistakes organizations can make right now is treating Copilot, AI, and agents as optional experiments.

What the interviews in this chapter show is that these tools are quickly moving from novelty to expectation.

Not everyone will use them in the same way. Not every role will adopt them at the same pace.

But the direction is clear.

As Copilot and AI-assisted tools become more common, the gap between people who know how to work with them, and those who don't, will widen.

AI As a Baseline Skill, Not a Specialty

In the early days, Copilot usage often feels like a personal advantage.

Someone writes faster.

Someone catches up on meetings more easily.

Someone produces better drafts with less effort.

Over time, those advantages stop being exceptional and start to become baseline expectations.

Just as knowing how to search, collaborate digitally, or work across systems has become a basic expected skill, the ability to work effectively with AI will increasingly be assumed.

Organizations that treat Copilot literacy as optional risk falling behind, not because the technology itself is perfect but because others are simply working with more leverage.

That same shift in expectations is even clearer when we talk about agents.

Agents As Leverage, Not Replacements

As agents become more common, it's tempting to frame them as stand-ins for human work.

But the reality is a bit more nuanced. I like to describe agents as force multipliers.

They amplify experience, domain knowledge, and judgment.

They don't replace them.

This is why agent adoption tends to benefit experienced practitioners first. People who understand what "good" looks like are better at guiding systems, spotting errors, and applying results appropriately.

You can see both the promise and the risks in viral projects like OpenClaw.

Watching an agent browse the web, send emails, schedule meetings, or automate multi-step tasks is genuinely impressive. It feels like a glimpse of what's coming.

It also exposes something uncomfortable.

A lot of people experimenting with these tools don't fully understand what they're connecting them to, or what could go wrong. Some are giving agents access to email, file systems, internal tools, and, in extreme cases, even financial accounts, without meaningful guardrails. Predictably, people have already lost money.

That doesn't mean agents are bad.

It means agents are powerful.

And power without structure is never a good idea.

Projects like OpenClaw tend to work best in the hands of people who understand permissions, boundaries, data sources, and failure modes. In other words, people who treat agents as systems that require design, not magic beings that "just figure things out."

You see a similar pattern in the hype around Moltbook, where people claim that agents creating posts, responding to each other, or exhibiting "personalities" means we've reached artificial general intelligence and are on the brink of machines taking over.

In reality, these agents are doing exactly what they were programmed to do: generate text based on prompts, memory, and interaction loops created by humans.

Interesting? Absolutely.

Proof of independent intelligence? Not really.

All of this reinforces the same point:

Give an agent broad access without structure, and you don't get a digital employee.

You get a system that can confidently do the wrong thing.

That's why agents aren't replacements for people.

They're tools that make capable people more effective when designed and governed responsibly.

Humans As Designers of Work Systems

As these tools mature, more people find themselves shaping *how* work gets done, not just doing the work itself.

They define

- What questions get asked

- What agents are allowed to do

- Where human review is required

- How outputs are used

This doesn't turn everyone into an engineer.

It turns many knowledge workers into **system designers at small scale.**

Some people refer to this as being an "agent boss." Others just call it good judgment.

Either way, the shift is real: people increasingly guide systems rather than operate them directly. Which brings us to the bigger question about jobs and the future of work.

A Realistic Future, Not a Magical One

If I had a dollar for every headline I've seen about AI replacing most jobs, I could probably retire early.

And I understand why those headlines resonate. Seeing CEOs and tech leaders publicly suggest that AI could automate almost all white-collar tasks within the next year or two is alarming.

I want to be clear: this is my personal perspective, based on what I see in real organizations. I don't buy that framing.

Not because AI, Copilot, and agents aren't powerful. They are. I use them daily. I build with them. I teach others how to use them. I also see their limits up close.

We've heard versions of this story before.

When cloud computing took off, we were told huge swaths of IT jobs would disappear.

When low-code platforms gained traction, we were told traditional development would shrink dramatically.

Meanwhile, many enterprises still run critical systems on AS/400 and mainframes.

C++ and COBOL developers are still in high demand.

Data quality is still a top problem almost everywhere I go.

Technology changes fast.

Organizations, processes, and incentives
change slowly.

AI will not replace all work. But it won't leave everything unchanged either.

In my view, the more realistic future looks like this: AI reshapes how work is done, not whether work exists. Some tasks get easier. Some disappear. New ones emerge. Most jobs become a mix of human judgment and machine assistance.

I'm not going to sugarcoat this. People are losing jobs. That's real, and it's painful. Whether a role disappears due to direct automation or because a company restructures after adopting AI, the reality for the people affected remains the same.

Where I tend to disagree with the loudest tech bro narratives is around scope.

I don't expect a future where entire occupations are suddenly wiped out because AI can now "do the job." What I see much more often is work being reshaped.

Tasks change.

Expectations change.

Productivity baselines move.

In many organizations, AI isn't making people work less. It's enabling people to take on more. And once that becomes possible, employers often expect it.

That's an uncomfortable truth.

So, the shift I pay attention to isn't "AI replaces humans."

It's "AI changes what humans are expected to handle."

That distinction doesn't make the transition easier.

But it does paint a more realistic picture than the idea of a mass extinction event for knowledge work.

So, when I think about the future, I don't see a world run by autonomous systems making most decisions on their own.

I see a world where

AI becomes another layer in the stack

Agents become another kind of tool

Humans remain responsible for judgment, context, and accountability.

Not magical.

Not dystopian.

Just different.

And very much still being figured out.

Summary and Key Takeaways

In this chapter, we moved beyond features and into reality. We looked at how Copilot and agents are being adopted inside organizations. We saw what works, what stalls, and what separates experimentation from sustained value. We explored common pitfalls like unrealistic expectations and poor data hygiene and examined the progression from simple search and drafting to standardized practices and operationalized agents. Most importantly, we reframed Copilot and agents not as magic automation tools, but as systems that amplify human judgment when they're grounded in good foundations.

Key Takeaways

- Copilot failures are more often expectation failures, not technology failures.

- The shift from "do this task" to "help me achieve this outcome" unlocks significantly better results.

- Data quality and knowledge organization matter more than clever prompts.

- Integrations and security configuration directly determine how useful Copilot can be.

- Communities and shared experimentation accelerate adoption more than formal training alone.

- Agents create the most value when they capture repeatable thinking processes, not vague ambitions.

- Mature adoption blends agents with workflows and keeps humans firmly in the loop.

- AI literacy is becoming a baseline skill, not a specialized advantage.

Index

A, B

Adoption
consistent pattern, 138
custom visuals/summaries, 140
editor and co-writer, 139
experimentation, 141–142
fancy search engine, 138–139
guardrails, 141
limitations, 139
maturity curve, 143
operationalization, 142–143
repeatability, 140
standardization, 140
trial and error, 141
Agents
approachable system, 81
approaches, 84
apps, 80–81
autonomous, 137
autonomous systems, 148
autonomy, 68
autopilot, 73
benefits, 88
builder, 96
building design, 88–89
categories, 91
conceptual level, 89
conversation, 81
data quality, 147
declarative (*see* Declarative
agents)
deterministic approaches, 69–70
differences, 72
events/schedules, 90–91
flows exist, 71
insurance company, 137
leverage, 145–146
low-code *vs.* pro-code, 87, 91
multiple tools, 74
objectives, 77
patterns, 81
personalities, 146
platforms, 80
primary interface, 79
product director, 136
realistic future, 148
responsible design
consideration, 78
retrieval agents, 137
retrieval process, 90
scenarios, 71–72
scenarios benefit, 74
task agents, 137
task-based agents, 90
time organizations, 136

Agents (*cont.*)
    trade-offs, 87
    workflows (*see* Workflows)
Analyst agents
    fundamentals, 14
    generalist/specialists, 13–14
    HR policy, 16
    IT support, 17
    low-code tools, 15
    pre-built agents, 15–17
    researcher, 15
    sales enablement, 16
Artificial intelligence (AI), 2
    assisted tools, 144
    automation, 67–68, 76, 83
    baseline expectations, 144
    deep learning, 25–26
    evolution, 29
    Gen AI (*see* Generative AI
        (Gen AI))
    machine learning, 24–25
    personal advantage, 144
    rule-based system, 22
Autonomous agents, 137

C

Chatbots
    approaches
        real-world scenario, 82
        traditional chatbot, 82
    conversational interfaces, 61
    human communication, 62
    intent, 62–63
    limitation, 66
    non-deterministic, 65–66
    patterns, 82
    scenarios, 75
    traditional, 64
    workflows (*see* Workflows)
ChatGPT, 27
Contextual prompt, 41
Copilot
    adoption, 138–143
    agents, 13
    AI (*see* Artificial intelligence (AI))
    assistive, 11
    concepts, 59
    cybersecurity and IT
        operations, 131
    different levels, 3
    digital transformation, 131
    ecosystem, 5–6
    enterprise-grade security, 7–8
    expectation failures, 127–128
    experiences, 10
    general-purpose AI, 6
    integrations, 131
    interface, 4
    licensing, 9
    multiple experiences, 5
    origin story, 1–2
    outcomes, 128
    platform, 84–85
    real procedures/standards, 130
    rule-based problem, 23
    security, 8–9, 131
    sounds different, 128–129

standardizaion, 4
training, 132–133
types, 126
user problem, 130–132
variation, 23
Copilot Studio, 108
   agent development platform, 108
   continuum, 111
   custom engine environment, 109
   declarative, 97, 109
   deployment, 110
   pro-code extensibility, 110
   real-world scenarios, 108
Custom engine agents
   approval process, 105
   audit environments, 106
   Copilot Studio, 108–111
   decision framework, 122
   explicit tool sequences, 105
   low-cost, 106
   meaning, 104
   multi-system, 105
   natural transition, 107
   ownership of, 107
   pro-code, 106
   scenarios, 103, 104

D

Decision framework, 17–18
   demand consistency, 122
   finance approval, 120–121
   HR policy/benefits
      questions, 117
   intelligence, 122
   onboarding assistant, 119–120
   ownership, 121–123
   requirements, 117
   sales organization, 118–119
Declarative agents, 99
   action model, 101
   approaches, 95
   builder, 96
   capabilities, 94
   Copilot Studio, 97, 108–111
   decision framework, 121–123
   deterministic workflow
      control, 100
   engine agents (*see* Custom
      engine agents)
   execution model, 98
   extensibility architecture, 102
   external systems, 100
   features, 101
   intent/boundaries, 93–94
   interaction, 99
   limitation, 102
   Microsoft 365 toolkit, 97
   orchestration (*see*
      Orchestration)
   pro-code, 111–117
   SharePoint permission model, 96
Deep learning, 25–26
Deterministic systems, 69

E

Expert systems, 22

F

Few-shot prompt, 41

G

Generalist, 13
Generative AI (Gen AI)
    categories, 28
    GPT series, 27
    pattern recognition-
        generation, 28
    rule-based systems, 28
    transformer architecture, 27
Generative Pre-trained
        Transformer (GPT),
        27, 51
GitHub Copilot, 1–2
Grounding
    accuracy, 50
    action, 49
    bounded access, 50
    flow process, 48, 49
    meaning, 48

H

Hallucination, 34–37
    core limitation, 37
    dramatic fictional
        invention, 35
    output verification, 36
    overview, 34
    specific details, 36

I, J, K

Intentional orchestration, 142

L

Large language models
        (LLMs), 21, 51
    chatbot, 65
    content type, 33
    declarative agents, 92
    emergent capabilities,
        31–32
    hallucination, 34–37
    learning process, 30–31
    limitations, 33
    overview, 29
    pattern-matching
        system, 32
    patterns, 30
Low-code agents, *see* Pro-
        code agents
Low-code tools, 15

M

Machine learning, 24–25
Microsoft 365, 11, 110

N

Neural networks, 25–26
Non-deterministic
        systems, 69

O

OpenClaw project, 145
Operationalization, 142–143
Orchestration, 87, 102
    Copilot Studio, 108–111
    decision framework, 121–123
    declarative agents, 94
    meaning, 92–94
    overview, 91
    workflow control, 100
Orchestration layer
    action, 54
    context, 55
    decision engine, 52
    desired output, 56
    information, 56
    leadership sections, 57
    models, 52
    multistep reasoning, 55
    outcome, 55
    output generation, 58
    reasoning/retrival, 57
    safety/compliance checks, 55
    simplest level, 53–54

P, Q

Pre-built agents, 15–17
Pro-code agents, 111
    benefits, 116
    capabilities, 116
    connectors/plugins, 114–115
    decision (*see* Decision
        framework)
    execution layer, 112
    extensibility model, 113
    external service, 115
    low-code capabilities, 112
    meaning, 112
    reliability, 114
    SDK-based agents, 113–114
    services, 114–115
    strategies, 116
Prompts
    effective, 43
    ingredients, 42–43
    instructions, 45
    interaction, 43–44
    overview, 40
    pattern types, 40–41
    spiral, 44
    traditional software, 40

R

Retrieval-augmented generation
        (RAG), 48
Retrieval-based agents, 137
Role-based prompt, 41
ROT (redundant, obsolete, and
        trivial data), 129

S

SharePoint agents, 96
Software development kits
        (SDKs), 113
Specialists, 13
System designers, 146

T

Task-based agents, 137
Tokens
    definition, 46
    environmental cost, 47
    life cycle, 46–47
Traditional chatbots, 64
Transformer
    architecture, 27

U, V

User interface (UI), 2

W, X, Y

Workflows
    AI automation, 67–68, 76
    approaches, 83
    approval process, 76
    capability, 70
    edges, 67
    execution, 66–67
Work systems, 146

Z

Zero-shot prompt, 41

GPSR Compliance
The European Union's (EU) General Product Safety Regulation (GPSR) is a set
of rules that requires consumer products to be safe and our obligations to
ensure this.

If you have any concerns about our products, you can contact us on

ProductSafety@springernature.com

In case Publisher is established outside the EU, the EU authorized
representative is:

Springer Nature Customer Service Center GmbH
Europaplatz 3
69115 Heidelberg, Germany